WEST POINT

*Whistler in Cadet Gray, and other
Stories about the United States
Military Academy*

by

KENNETH W. RAPP

NORTH RIVER PRESS

CLOTHBOUND ISBN 0-88427-031-9
PAPERBACK ISBN 0-88427-032-7

Library of Congress Catalog Card No. 78-61828

CREDITS

All drawings and photographs are from the collections of the United States Military Academy.

The story of Fanny Elssler on page 15 is reprinted by courtesy of *Dance Magazine*.

This book would not have been possible without the support and encouragement of the Daughters of the United States Army (DUSA).

Manufactured in the United States of America

WEST POINT

CONTENTS

PREFACE & ACKNOWLEDGEMENTS

The purpose of this small book of early West Point lore is twofold. First, it is intended to make known to the general public the rich resources contained in the U.S. Military Academy Archives at West Point, New York. Secondly, it will provide the increasing annual influx of tourists who visit the beautiful grounds at the Military Academy with a small momento of their brief stay at West Point.

The author has attempted to record a number of human interest stories and illustrate them appropriately. It is his hope that his efforts will familiarize the reader with a small portion of the history of the Military Academy, its graduates, and former cadets.

The stories which follow concern a few unique graduates and ex-cadets, and the circumstances surrounding the visits of three celebrated figures to the renowned military institution; they also provide an insight into a few of the little known Academy origins, legends, and traditions. All of these contributed in a small way to making America the great nation that it so rightfully is.

To my wife, Dorothy M. Rapp, I owe the most gratitude. Without her continued encouragement and support this bit of West Point lore might never have reached completion.

The assistance of Mr. Stanley P. Tozeski is sincerely appreciated. His kind interest in making certain editorial suggestions to improve the readability of the manuscript is gratefully acknowledged.

I am also deeply indebted to Miss Mary Piccone and Mrs. Regina M. Hanretta. Their aid in typing the manuscript and their thoughtfulness and many kindnesses to me will always be appreciated.

I would be remiss if I failed to cite the following agencies at the U.S. Military Academy who furnished me with invaluable assistance: the USMA Archives, the Special Collections Division of the West Point Library, the West Point Museum, and the Public Affairs Office.

The encouragement and courtesies of the following publications and organizations are also gratefully appreciated by the author: *Assembly*, a publication of The Association of Graduates Office, UMSA; *The Newburgh Evening News*, Newburgh, N.Y.; *The Times-Herald Record* of Middletown, N.Y.; and *The Grabhorn-Hoyem Press* of San Francisco, California for granting me permission to use the Derby cartoon, and the portion of Derby's humorous style of writing on the composition of armies which accompanies the Derby story in this volume.

Finally, I dedicate this booklet to my daughter, Jean Marie Rapp, who is as truly American as any American can possibly be!

INTRODUCTION

That An Army of Asses Led By A Lion Is Vastly Superior To
An Army Of Lions Led By An Ass. (A favorite saying of
General Washington)

During the American Revolution, the colonists had few edu-
cated officers, and as a result, were frequently dependent upon
European soldiers of fortune, who were eagerly employed with
high rank and extravagant pay. The problem of inadequate
officers in the army was best described by General Charles Lee
who stated, "We had not an officer in the Army who knew the
difference betwixt a Chevaux-de-frise and a cabbage-garden."

General Washington and other patriotic statesmen were
aware of the drastic situation and felt that a national school for
the education of capable officers was mandatory. Their arduous
efforts were realized when the U.S. Military Academy was
established in 1802.

The mission of the U.S. Military Academy is "to educate,
train and motivate the Corps of Cadets so that each graduate
shall have the character, leadership, and other attributes
essential to progressive and continuing development throughout
a career of exemplary service to the Nation as an officer of the
Regular Army."

Through the years the past administrations at the Military
Academy have done exceedingly well in accomplishing this
mission. Such names as Pershing, Sherman, Clark, Patch, and
Patton attest to the soundness of the military program in
providing superb military leadership to our country in times of
crises.

In addition, there have been many cadets who for one
reason or another were not able to remain at the Academy to
complete their cadetships and receive their commissions in the
U.S. Army. An analysis of the large roster of these former

1

Mount Vernon, December 12: 1799

Sir,

I have duly received your letter of the 28th ultimo, enclosing a copy of what you had written to the Secretary of War, on the subject of a Military Academy.

The Establishment of an Institution of this kind, upon a respectable and extensive basis, has ever been considered by me as an Object of primary importance to this Country; — and while I was in the Chair of Government I omitted no proper opportunity of recommending it, in my public Speeches, and otherways, to the attention of the Legislature: — But I never undertook to go into a detail of the organization of such an Academy; leaving this task to others, whose pursuits in the paths of Science, and attention to the arrangements of such Institutions, had better qualified them for the execution of it. —

For the same reason I must now decline making any observations on the details of your plan; — and as it has already been submitted to the Secretary of War, through whom it would naturally be laid before Congress, it might be too late for alterations if any should be suggested.

I sincerely hope that the subject will meet with due attention, and that the reasons for its establishment, which you have so clearly pointed out in your letter to the Secretary, will prevail upon the Legislature to place it upon a permanent and respectable footing. —

With very great esteem & regard,
I am, Sir,
Your most obed.t Serv.t
G Washington

General Hamilton

Letter from President George Washington to Alexander Hamilton expressing the thoughts of the President on the creation of the U.S. Military Academy just two days before the President's death.

cadets reveals that all were not lost in vain. For example, a large number of ex-cadets have made significant contributions in other fields of endeavor and have played important roles in providing America with dedicated leadership and in advancing her cultural interests throughout the world. An examination of the Casualty Books in the USMA Archives indicated that such former cadets as Edgar Allan Poe and James A.M. Whistler carved their mark in the literary and art worlds. Ex-cadets William Gilpin and Benjamin G. Humphreys became governors of the states of Colorado and Mississippi. Nicholas P. Trist, ex-cadet of the Class of 1822, became prominent in the diplomatic and legal profession. Trist had been the chief clerk in the Department of State and in the absence of Secretary of State James Buchanan during the mid 1840's occasionally acted as the head of the department.

It is also interesting to note that a number of former cadets were recipients of the coveted Congressional Medal of Honor, one of the most recent being Captain Roger H. Donlon, ex-Class of 1959. Captain Donlon was the first receiver of the award after the Korean War.

And last but certainly not least, it is of passing interest to note that ex-cadets Andrew H. Foote, James F. Schenck, and Henry Knox Thatcher (Grandson of General Henry Knox of Revolutionary fame) became worthy admirals in the damned U.S. Navy!

WHISTLER IN CADET GRAY

An episode in the Early Life of an American Artist

On a hot, humid day in July 1851, a rather slight young lad named James McNeill Whistler reported for admission to the United States Military Academy at West Point, New York.

Little did he know then of the travail he would experience as a cadet or that his stay at West Point would end three years hence — just one year short of graduation. Why did Whistler's cadet career in the Class of 1855 come to a close when it did in 1854?

Some of the answers can be found in the West Point archives. Documents, writings, letters, books, and even a doctor's certificate dated July 8, 1854, reveal much of the Whistler story. All these sources put into perspective the ordeal and the luster of a notable American artist.

The record shows that when Whistler entered the Military Academy in 1851, a second classman named Cadet William R. Boggs was adjutant of the Corps of Cadets. Boggs knew much about the accomplishments of young Whistler's father, George W. Whistler, Class of 1819, who had gained recognition as the engineer who built a railroad in Russia. Boggs's regard for engineering and his admiration for the elder Whistler prompted him to befriend the new plebe quickly.

In the course of time, Boggs began to notice that whenever Whistler had a few spare moments in his busy cadet schedule he would invariably pick up his pen and some scrap paper and start making character sketches of cadets. Impressed by Whistler's drawings, Boggs became so enthusiastic that he showed a few of them to other cadets. He often remarked that Whistler probably would not remain at the Military Academy to graduate since it appeared to him Whistler was destined to be an artist of note.

United States Military Academy.

West Point N.Y. July 1st 1851

I James A. Whistler of the State of Connecticut aged Sixteen years, & Eleven months, having been selected for an appointment as Cadet in the Military Academy of the United States, do hereby engage, with the consent of my Mother in the event of my receiving such appointment, that I will serve in the army of the United States for eight years unless sooner discharged by competent Authority. And I James A. Whistler do solemnly swear, that I will bear true faith and allegiance to the United States of America, and that I will serve them honestly and faithfully against all their enemies or opposers whomsoever; and that I will observe and obey the orders of the President of the United States, and orders of the Officers appointed over me, according to the Rules and Articles of War.

J. Whistler.

Sworn and subscribed to, at West Point N.Y. this 7th day of February 1852 before me Robt Proudfit

Special County Judge of Orange County N.Y.

Engagement for Service and Oath of Allegiance signed by Cadet Whistler.

History has shown how prophetic was his judgement. It also has shown that Whistler's attendance at West Point was due solely to the influence of his distinguished father and that of his eminent uncle, Major William G. McNeill, in the Class of 1817. Both had brilliant careers in their country's service, and both had attained fame as early pioneers in the American railroad industry. It was therefore, undoubtedly the wish of Anna Whistler that her son James should follow them in the military profession. She was delighted with her son's drawing talent, but did not think a career in that field would be in his best interests. The decision whether her son should don Cadet Gray was hers to make, since her husband had died at St. Petersburg, Russia in April, 1849. They had enjoyed both the comforts and security of Army life, and she wanted her son to have the same privileges.

Whistler lived at Pomfret, Connecticut when he was appointed to the Military Academy by President Millard Fillmore. Entering this new and entirely different phase of his life, he quickly became acquainted with his classmates. Among them were many young men who, in various fields, later carved their mark in American history. These included Alexander S. Webb whose personal gallantry at the Battle of Gettysburg later earned for him the Medal of Honor, and William W. Averell and David M. Gregg who after graduation gained fame as noted Indian fighters, and who served with distinction in the Civil War, both reaching the rank of brevet major general. Two of Whistler's classmates later became prominent in the diplomatic field. Gregg, in addition to his military achievements, was later appointed U.S. consul to Prague. Alfred T. Torbert became the United States minister to Salvador and was subsequently appointed the consul general to Paris in 1873.

Whistler's cadet life turned out to be a stormy one. Academically, although he stood relatively low in Mathematics and English, he excelled in French and Drawing. The military side of his cadet career however was a real problem. He had an extremely difficult time adhering to the strict discipline required and administered at West Point.

A volume of *The Register of Delinquencies* covering the period of Whistler's cadetship reveals that he committed many minor infractions which would normally have been overlooked

First Half Hour

Second Half Hour

Sketches on this and following page were drawn by Cadet Whistler and titled "On Post in Camp." They show the progress of a bored cadet in two hours on post.

Third Half Hour

Last Half Hour!

at other schools. During his Plebe year, for example, he received demerits for talking in ranks at drill, for loitering in the commandant's office during the absence of the commandant, and for neglecting the care of a class model in the Drawing Academy.

Delinquencies recorded in his Yearling year included: failure to salute the officer of the day properly, loitering in the Drawing Academy, carelessness in mounting his horse, and leaving the Drawing Academy before the expiration of two hours.

An interesting incident occurred in his second year and is particularly worthy of mention. Cadet Whistler and his roommate, Henry M. Lazelle, were placed in arrest for playing cards. The report of the commandant of cadets states they were discovered sitting in their room at a table covered with playing cards. Interestingly enough, Whistler was caught "red handed" because he was observed with the cards in his hands. The incident proved to be rather ironic since Lazelle graduated with his class and later served as commandant of cadets during the years 1879-82.

During his third and final year, Cadet Whistler was cited, among other things, for singing and talking aloud in the Drawing Academy, for being off limits while skating on the Hudson River, for having long hair at inspection, and for exchanging his horse on the road without permission.

There is no doubt that Whistler understood the subject, but from the infractions committed in Drawing one can only surmise that he had very little real interest in becoming an officer in the United States Army.

Another unfortunate circumstance may also have led to Whistler's departure from the Military Academy. He had suffered from rheumatic attacks as a young boy. In May 1853 during his Yearling year at West Point, Cadet Whistler was taken ill with such an attack. This prompted Colonel Robert E. Lee, then Superintendent of the Military Academy, to send a letter to Mrs. Whistler informing her of Whistler's illness.

In the letter, Lee stated that Cadet Whistler was not suffering much pain, but also that his attack did not seem to be responding to treatment, and the West Point surgeon feared the boy's lungs were seriously injured. He concluded the letter by assuring Mrs. Whistler that her son would receive every attention and treatment which it was in his power to bestow. A copy of Mrs. Whistler's poignant reply to Colonel Lee was recently found in the Archives.

Four days after Lee's letter was sent to his mother, Cadet Whistler was given a leave of absence for medical reasons.

A second letter, this one written by Cadet Whistler, has also been uncovered in the Archives. Addressed to the adjutant of the post, it concerned the requirement to submit a doctor's certificate justifying his leave for reasons of health. It was written from his mother's home in Scarsdale, New York, and was dated July 7, 1853. Mrs. Whistler had moved to Scarsdale from Pomfret, Connecticut, to be closer to her sons, James at West Point and William, who was about to enter Columbia College in New York City. The letter reveals that Whistler was in somewhat of a quandary regarding the proper form he should use in submitting a doctor's certificate to account for his absence from the post. It implies that he was highly perturbed because he had not received a letter from the adjutant explaining the course of action he should take in submitting the certificate. Whistler emphasized strongly that he could not understand how a note directed to Scarsdale, New York, could possibly miscarry.

Whistler finally submitted the certificate to Colonel Lee on July 20, 1853. It stated that a Dr. Camman had thoroughly examined Whistler and, having diagnosed his disease as endocarditis, urged the utmost caution to prevent a recurrence of its acute symptoms. Dr. Camman also remarked that exposure or imprudence would frequently cause the cardiac condition to reappear with increased violence.

Whistler remained on convalescent leave until the 28th of August, when he resumed his cadet career. However, after a short time he had again run afoul of the disciplinary system at West Point. His demerits continued to rise at a rapid rate. At the same time, he began to encounter difficulty in his chemistry course. After being termed deficient in chemistry, Whistler is reported to have said, "Had silicon been a gas, I would have been a major general."

In less than a year after his return from sick leave, Whistler's cadetship was ended. Nevertheless, despite his official discharge, Whistler tried to complete his West Point career. He submitted an application for readmission to General Joseph G. Totten, the chief engineer of the Army, who had control over the administration of the Military Academy. General Totten, in turn, forwarded the application to Colonel Robert E. Lee, who in a most profound manner, pointed out that he could do nothing more on Whistler's behalf. The superintendent summarized Whistler's cadet career by saying: "I can only regret that one so capable of doing well should so have neglected himself and must now suffer the penalty."

Whistler had exceeded the authorized number of demerits administered for infractions of military discipline. He was unable to adhere to the established standards for cadet life and discipline at West Point, and he fell victim to the demerit system. The term "Conduct" has always been the official title of this system, and even today it is the method used to evaluate a cadet's performance of routine duties.

His three years as a cadet at the Military Academy could be considered by some as an insignificant phase of Whistler's life. The renowned artist, however, always regarded it as a very meaningful part of his life. He never forgot that he had once been a member of the Corps of Cadets. An inscription on the title page of a book which he presented to the United States Military Academy Library reads: "From An Old Cadet, Whose Pride is to Remember His West Point Days."

After leaving the Military Academy, Whistler was somewhat unsettled. Eventually, he accepted a position as draftsman with the Coast Survey in Washington, D.C., and served in that capacity for one year. He soon realized, however, that the only way he could achieve true happiness in life was to devote himself completely to art. His decision proved to be wise and rewarding.

Whistler's great works received notable recognition, but not before many bitter struggles with art critics and his own countrymen. After gaining fame, it was apparently for this reason that he wanted revenge against the critics and everyone who had scorned him earlier. He achieved his revenge by conveying the impression that he was abnormally conceited. This is best illustrated by an episode which took place later in his life at a time that saw his undisputed genius preserved on canvas.

One morning, a pupil in his art class greeted him by saying: "Oh, Mr. Whistler, coming in on the train this morning the countryside was shrouded with a beautiful soft haze; and everywhere I looked I seemed to see in the landscape one of your charming paintings."

"Yes, yes," said Whistler, with exaggerated pomposity, "Nature's creeping up! She's creeping up!"

Whistler's words also tell us there was not a hint of doubt in his mind or heart that he had found his true station in life, and he fulfilled it to the limit of his abilities.

When he came to West Point, it appeared that he was destined to be a soldier. But aspiration and inner God-given talents led him instead to become one of the world's most acclaimed artists. His works will live through the ages; and the Army's loss, in this case, was the entire world's gain.

FANNY ELSSLER'S PIROUETTE BY MOONLIGHT

A Legend

Without dreams, man's life is but a jest, a shadow, a bubble, air, gone before we realize it. (Justin G. Turner, *Manuscripts*, Spring 1967)

The above quotation is certainly applicable to the life of a cadet at the United States Military Academy. From the day of entry into the Academy the new plebe is constantly under strict regimentation and discipline. He is kept busy from reveille to taps with calisthenics, drills, orientation and academics. The individual cadet, therefore, must find a few spare moments for relaxation and fun in order to retain his sanity. This was especially true at the Academy during the 1840s.

During that early period a former cadet wrote a summary of a supposed event which has turned into one of the slickest legends in West Point history. It has been said that a well-established, well-beloved legend is at once the joy of a people and the despair of the historian. It has just enough truth in it to be convincing, and not quite enough to be factual.

This story had its origin at the Military Academy on August 4, 1840. On that date Miss Fanny Elssler and her party arrived at the old West Point Hotel after sailing up the majestic Hudson River on the evening boat. Miss Elssler was the toast of Europe and probably at that time the world's greatest ballerina. She was born in Vienna, Austria in 1810 and began her dancing career six years later. At the age of seventeen she performed with her older sister in Naples, and she subsequently appeared throughout Europe in such major cities as Berlin, London, and Paris.

Fanny was especially admired for her grace, agility and beauty. Her performances caused considerable excitement among the patrons of the theaters of Paris; her engagements, witnessed by royalty throughout all of Europe, brought her international fame. It was because of this reputation and dancing ability that the theatergoers in the United States clamored to see her perform. Their wishes were granted in the spring of 1840 when she consented to visit the country on a two-year tour. Before her arrival at West Point she had performed in Washington, where so many senators wished to attend her performances that it was necessary to adjourn Congress! Fanny had the distinction of being received at the White House by President Martin Van Buren and his cabinet; and a banquet was held in her honor at which a toast was drunk from one of her slippers. Reports even claimed that the sedate city of Boston relented to Fanny's overall charm. It was in Boston that she gave a benefit performance for the unfinished Bunker Hill Monument. As a result of this engagement, the story goes, a pair of her ballet slippers was placed in the cornerstone. Based on these reports, it is easy to understand why the young gentlemen at the Military Academy were so impatient to see such a beauty on the grounds of West Point.

The stage is now set to recount the humorous but little-known Academy legend concerning the ballerina. The setting was Fort Clinton, where the summer encampment of the Corps of Cadets was held each year. The encampment consisted of sixty-to-eighty white tents; in appearance it was a little community divided by four streets. The outermost limits of the encampment were marked by a chain of eight sentinel posts. A small octagonal frame watch-house, which could be occupied by the guard during inclement weather, stood at each post. It was at such posts that the cadet sentinels walked off their tours of guard duty, and these tours were in all probability particularly lonely on beautiful, moonlit, summer nights.

The main character of the legend was, of course, the famed Fanny Elssler, but a lowly cadet named Pierre Dubois played the leading male role in our story.

Fanny's presence on post created a tremendous stir of interest among the cadets. Normally, the spring season turns a young man's fancy to love; in this instance, however, the young cadet

Fanny Elssler was the subject of many 19th century lithographs.

View of the Hudson River from West Point, c1837. Engraving by R. Wallis, based on painting by W.H. Bartlett.

View of the Military Academy as Fanny Elssler might have seen it. From an original water color by Augustus Kollner.

hearts were reeling in August. Fanny's planned two-day retreat to West Point had a definite effect on the entire corps. Each cadet became noticeably meticulous in overall appearance. Additionally, the smart execution of soldierly duties became more apparent. Each cadet undoubtedly felt that the beautiful, blue eyes of the "maitresse du ballet" were witnessing his every movement. As evening approached a committee of cadets decided to hold a special dance, and assembled an orchestra of drums, fifes and violins.

This stag dance was composed of approximately fifty couples of youthful cadets, each doing its best to gain highest recognition from the citizen spectators witnessing the event. This social (secretly arranged for Fanny) turned out to be one of her most memorable evenings on her extended tour of the United States.

At the conclusion of the dance, the cadets were required to return to their tents. The regulations at that time stated that no one could cross the line of posts after ten o'clock at night without giving the sentinel the proper password, if challenged to do so. Unfortunately, poor Cadet Pierre Dubois, together with a select group of other cadets, had the misfortune of drawing the guard duty for the evening. They were prevented from feasting their eyes on the lovely dancer and were most perturbed. Fortunately for Cadet Dubois his opportunity was to come later in the evening.

It was a particularly warm and humid evening, Fanny and her escort, Monsieur Sylveste, decided to take a leisurely stroll. Dubois had been assigned to guard duty at Post Number Five situated in a remote area on the northern end of what is known today as Flirtation Walk. In such a desolate location it was not unusual for the cadet on guard to take an occasional cat nap with little chance of being detected.

On this seemingly quiet night one can well imagine the thoughts that crossed Pierre's mind as he secretly gazed upon the ravishing beauty from a screened position. His train of thought instantly suggested a plot which was at once daring and humorous. To appreciate the full human interest of the incident and to memorialize the charming wit of Cadet Pierre Dubois, here is how that enterprising cadet reported it:

"Halt! Who comes there?" cried Dubois in bloodcurdling tones.

"Does Monsieur speak to us?" asked M. Sylveste apprehensively.

"Advance and give the countersign," growled the sentry, bringing his musket down to a charge.

The gallant escort took to his heels and fled ingloriously, leaving the trembling Fanny before the terrible man of war.

"Ze countersign; vat is dat?" she asked.

"The passe parole," answered the sentinel.

"Helas! I have it not. I will send to the commandant, and my servant shall bring it to you, demain, in the morning."

"Madam!" shouted Dubois, "have you dared to pass my post without the countersign?"

"Oh, sare, I did not know."

The other sentinels knew that something was up, and, enveloped in their huge guard cloaks, deserted their posts, to range themselves alongside Dubois. They encouraged him to carry on the joke, and he immediately indulged in a lengthy harangue upon the terrible nature of her crime, and ending by informing her that death was the penalty then and there.

"Mais, Monsieur, s'il vous plait, do you know me? Je suis Mlle. Elssler, la pauvre Elssler."

Thinking she saw the effect of her declaration, she continued in an impassioned way:

"Oui, Monsieur, je suis la jollie, gayuse Fanny, je vous assure."

"Madam," replied Dubois, "by making any terms, by accepting an excuse for your crime, I render myself liable to court martial and instant death; but there is one condition, and only one, whereby you may atone for your offense against the flag of my country and save your wretched life."

"Mais, la condition, la condition, I will perform it."

"And that is, that you will here, in this solemn presence, within sight of yon gleaming monument of the Polish chieftain, dance the Cracovienne."

"Sacre, pose, mon Dieu! C'est impossible!" cried the now indignant Fanny.

"Then die, proud female!" was the reply.

"But messieurs, I would dance avec plaisir, mais; vare is de-orchestra, de trombone, de flute, de feedle? I cannot dance widout de musique."

"The music shall be provided, madame; I will whistle."

"Jamais, jamais, monsieur," she cried, trembling with indignation and fright.

"Then," cried Dubois, "you know the awful penalty; prepare for your doom."

The guards gathered around in a ghostly way, while Dubois brought his piece down to a ready.

"Ah, me, gentilhommes, I will dance."

The guns were stacked, and with difficulty Dubois brought his mouth to a pucker and whistled the Cracovienne, while the graceful Fanny, lifting her skirts to keep them from the dew, executed the pirouette with infinite grace. When she had given the last kick and was about to retire they called for the Cachucha.

"Second relief, turn out!" cried the corporal of the guards, as he brought the butt of his musket down to awaken the guard. Instantly the sentinels ran to their posts, and Fanny started for the hotel like a frightened deer. On the way she met M. Sylveste, at the head of a mob of waiters armed with brooms, mops and pokers. She explained that his gallantry might have been shown earlier in the evening, and turned the crowd toward the hotel. It was said that Fanny and her party left before daylight, so the first relief of the guards were the only ones at the Point who had the opportunity of witnessing the fascinating beauty of the Cracovienne.

Naturally, after examining the account of Fanny Elssler's tragic experience with the cadet guards, the author became curious as to how much of the story was factual and how much was myth. Sources were checked for information concerning Cadet Pierre Dubois. This, as expected, turned out to be fruitless. It was frustrating to find not a single source to furnish the slightest clue as to who Pierre Dubois actually was. Another question raised was, "Did the famous ballerina really visit the military academy?"

If she didn't, why would a former cadet write such a descriptive summary of her stay?

An examination of early newspapers in the USMA Library collection confirmed that Fanny Elssler did indeed tour the United States in the early 1840s. The register of guests at the West Point Hotel confirmed that Elssler and party registered at the hotel on August 4, 1840. Continued search for the identity of Cadet Pierre Dubois eventually disclosed that a former cadet named George Michael Wharton was the real Pierre Dubois, the scoundrel who insisted that Fanny perform the Cracovienne on that beautiful moonlit night in August, 1840. Verification of this fact came from a letter written by a Mr. Frederick Dreyfus, an astute scholar of Wharton Family history, to Miss Thelma Bedell, the former chief reference librarian at the Military Academy in 1950.

George M. Wharton, alias Pierre Dubois, was admitted to the Academy on July 1, 1841 and resigned on May 25, 1843 because of a "deficiency in conduct." This bit of information confirmed that Fanny Elssler's pirouette by moonlight was pure myth. Since Fanny arrived at West Point in August of 1840 it was impossible that Wharton (alias Pierre Dubois) who entered in July of 1841, could have subjected Fanny to such harassment.

Subsequent to his service as a cadet, which was not at all to his liking, Wharton decided to enter the practice of medicine. His father was a prominent physician in Tuscumbia, Alabama, and the family persuaded young George to follow in his footsteps. He attended the New York University Medical School and was graduated in 1847. He then returned to Tuscumbia and opened his practice among old friends and acquaintances. During his leisure hours he relaxed by engaging in literary writing.

His writings were greatly admired in the South, and because of this natural talent and flair for humorous composition, he decided to drop his medical practice. Wharton then accepted a position as a writer on the staff of the *New Orleans Weekly Delta*. According to a volume entitled *The Life and Works of George Michael Wharton*, by Frederick Dreyfus, his career as a writer was short-lived. In May 1853 the city of New Orleans experienced one of the worst yellow fever epidemics in history. Dr. Wharton returned quickly to his profession to care for the sick. In less than six months he too was stricken with the disease and died in August of that year.

As a final tribute to Dr. Wharton, *The North Alabamian* of Tuscumbia printed the following eulogy:

Poor George! — and this is the end of all his cherished dreams, of ambitions and longings after wordly reputation and fame! . . . Like most men of poetic turn of mind, George was a dreamer — a builder of fairy castles — which are too frequently resolved into their original elements, air, upon the approach of reality. But he was possessed of genius — real genius — which, had he been spared to the usually alloted age of man, would have made itself known and appreciated."

This story of Fanny Elssler's brief visit to the U.S. Military Academy was published in *Dance Magazine* in July 1975. It was one of two feature articles selected by that magazine to open a series of Bicentennial articles celebrating the history of American dance. It is reprinted here to emphasize the fact that West Pointers not only left their mark in the arts of warfare, but in other fields as well. Although former Cadet George M. Wharton never achieved the fame of fellow cadets Edgar Allen Poe and Charles King, Jr., he too seems to have had a natural talent for fiction!

THE BRITISH TOOK WEST POINT —
DRAMATICALLY

West Point was captured — not by the British in the American Revolution, no thanks to Benedict Arnold. It was a century later that the British did succeed — but it was an acting troupe that pulled it off.

On March 19, 1888, Sir Henry Irving, one of the greatest of all English Shakespearean actors, arranged to have his Lyceum Theater group perform for the enjoyment of the U.S. Corps of Cadets at West Point. The date is of considerable interest because it was the first appearance of a professionally trained theatrical group at West Point since the founding of the U.S. Military Academy in 1802.

Prior to the celebrated event, the cadets lived a rather sheltered life. Their sole relief from the monotonous military routine consisted of the usual Saturday evening hops or an occasional minstrel show. In all probability the only exceptions, and certainly most enjoyable events, were humorous lectures delivered by Mark Twain, a frequent visitor in the early 1880s, who had the cadets and post personnel rolling in the aisles with laughter.

Sir Henry Irving had already received considerable acclaim throughout Europe when he arrived in the United States from London in the spring of 1888. Brilliant performances by his unique theater group at the Star Theater in New York City soon began to receive national attention.

Irving had expressed a keen interest in the Military Academy since his first informal visit to America several years earlier. At that time his hope had been to bring his entire company to West Point for a grand Shakespearean play. He reluctantly decided against it, however, since he felt it would be too difficult to obtain official permission from the military authorities. Nevertheless, his expressions of interest were eventually rewarded, and his wish was finally granted by Superintendent John G. Parke.

Sir Henry proceeded to implement his plan of action by making arrangements with the president of the West Shore Railroad Company to transport his entire cast from New York City to West Point. He had selected one of Shakespeare's better known plays, "The Merchant of Venice," as the performance of the evening.

A special stage was erected in the Mess Hall and, on the evening of the performance, the hall was filled to capacity. The young cadets were especially anxious to see the celebrated Ellen Terry, then Irving's leading lady in all his presentations.

The *New York Herald* for the period gave the following summary of the evening's performance:

Mr. Irving never revealed his genius as an actor more completely than he did last night as Shylock, or Miss Terry as Portia never appeared more wholly winsome, charming, and magnetic. Perhaps it is to the audience that this magnificent exhibition of the entire company's powers is to be ascribed, for a more appreciative audience never sat through a performance. Such an audience cannot be passed lightly over. Indeed its quality deserves special emphasis. Two hundred and fifty cadets encased in the regulation gray, tight fitting coats, ornamented by double rows of buttons, about their necks round, stiff white collars, and holding their caps in their white-gloved hands, filled row after row of the front seats. Never did the cadets look better, and recognizing the treat in store for them as something extraordinary, their faces beamed with happy expectancy. Every good point, every line was received with the quickness and spontaniety of applause that indicated not only intelligence, but minds, which, if not trained, were subject to the process of it. When the curtain fell the cadets cheered until the room fairly shook. They tossed their caps to the ceiling. It was a tremendous ovation.

After a brief pause, Mr. Irving appeared in evening dress and thanked the audience for their attention, and closed a happy and brief address by remarking, "I believe the joy bells are now ringing in London because a British Army has for the first time captured West Point!"

As a tribute to Miss Terry's acting talents, the Class of 1889 expressed its appreciation by inviting her to attend the graduation exercises the following year.

Sir Henry Irving as Shylock, the role he played in the historic West Point appearance.

The comment by Irving concerning the capture of West Point naturally has aroused local curiosity. An examination of documents in the USMA Archives turned up some fascinating letters which describe the close association between Irving and the authorities at West Point.

On March 20, the day following the historical performance, Superintendent Parke wrote to Irving who had returned to the Brunswick Hotel in New York City. Parke expressed his gratitude on behalf of the Corps of Cadets for the great and unprecedented performance.

He also stated how Irving certainly "touched a chord, the vibrations of which extend to every district in our broad land," and he said he was sure that "a life-long impression was made on those young minds which could never be effaced."

A few days later General Parke received the following response from Irving:

Dear General Parke:

I cannot express to you the delight which it gave Miss Terry and myself & our company to play to that splendid audience on Monday. I remember no privilege which we appreciate more & I am sure we shall never play the 'Merchant of Venice' again, without thinking how every passage was received by the West Point Cadets. And no success that we may achieve at any time can ever be remembered by those young hearts & that one memorable evening will dwell as long with them as it will with us.

A thousand thanks to you, General for your courtesy & good wishes. Believe me that on the sea & at home in England, you will, all of you, be present in our affectionate regard.

Ever, my dear General,

Sincerely & Respectfully yours,
HENRY IRVING

Coverage of the historic event by news correspondents of the day revealed its true significance to the U.S. Military Academy and to the American theatrical profession.

It was of particular importance to the cadets and staff at West Point because it was the first appearance of a professionally trained theatrical group at that institution.

Secondly, it demonstrated the excellent character and genuine sincerity of the Shakespearean actor, Sir Henry Irving. How many distinguished actors or theater managers would close their

Ellen Terry as Portia, the role she played in Shakespeare's "Merchant of Venice."

own theater for a night and accept the financial loss from a cancelled engagement?

Additionally, as one reporter remarked, "the actor and manager who will give the performance of a play for the pure love and affection of Shakespeare, is a conspicuously noticeable personage."

Irving's successful venture to West Point set a precedent which was followed eighteen years later by another famous Shakespearean group. The performers, directed by the noted Ben Greet, presented the play, "As You Like It," on June 27, 1906.

One of the fine young actors Greet had under his direction was Sydney Greenstreet, later a famous Hollywood star, who portrayed the banished duke in the play. Greenstreet had begun his theatrical career with the Ben Greet School of Acting in London in 1902.

The delightful experience that began with Sir Henry Irving's Lyceum Theater Players in 1888 and continued through the years with other famous Shakespearean groups still generates tremendous interest within the Corps of Cadets.

There is a passage in Shakespeare's play, "King Richard II," which reads as follows:

"As in a theatre, the eyes of men,
After a well-graced actor leaves the stage,
Are idly bent on him that enters next,
Thinking his prattle to be tedious."

Henry Irving could very well have been the type of "well-graced actor" alluded to by Shakespeare. Irving died in London, England on October 13, 1905. Tributes to the brilliant actor and gentleman were received from people the world over.

At the time, the Superintendent of the Military Academy, Brigadier General Albert L. Mills, expressed the sympathy of the officers and cadets. Writing to Bram Stoker, the manager of the Lyceum Theater in London, on November 15, 1905, Mills remarked how everyone at West Point appreciated the high qualities of mind and heart shown by the great actor whom England had so honored.

Mills concluded his letter by stating, "We desire to pay this tribute to his memory in unison with the many individuals and organizations throughout the world whom he has charmed by his personal qualities and delighted by his histrionic genius."

West Point and the U.S. Military Academy are steeped in tradition and legend, and yet little is known of the charitable and gracious act performed by Sir Henry Irving.

In a sense, his visit, which caused a great impact on the minds of the young cadets, also proved to be a forerunner in providing the corps with a new form of culture.

THE HISTORY OF DANCING AT THE U.S. MILITARY ACADEMY

I have often said that if I were compelled to have one required
subject in Harvard College, I would make it dancing if I could.
West Point has been very wise in this respect, and I am inclined
to think that Annapolis has had the same policy. (Charles W.
Eliot, President of Harvard University, 1869-1909)

Formal instruction in the art of dancing was first introduced to
the cadets with the hiring of a "dancing master" in 1823. Actually, dancing at West Point predated the Military Academy by
approximately twenty years. Prior to the establishment of the
Academy in 1802, the Post of West Point, which is today the
oldest continuously garrisoned post in America, was the scene
of numerous fancy and historic balls. One of the earliest balls at
West Point was the celebration of the birth of Dauphin of
France, held at West Point on May 31, 1782. The all-day affair
was filled with various exercises and activities. Later in the evening a great display of fireworks was witnessed by American
Generals Washington and Knox, and the famous French General
Lafayette. Immediately following the fireworks display, a
splendid ball was held and, as reported in *Thatcher's Journal*,
"the ball-room was an immense arbour erected for the purpose
on the plain which is now the parade ground for the cadets. His
Excellency, General Washington, with a dignified and graceful
air, having Mrs. Knox for his partner, carried down a dance of
twenty couples in the arbour on the green grass."

The initial impetus which eventually led to formal instruction in dancing for the Corps of Cadets came as early as April,
1783. The noted Baron von Steuben, in his scheme for the
organization of a national military academy, submitted a plan
to General Washington recommending that horsemanship, fenc-

ing, dancing, and music be made a part of the regular curriculum. Unfortunately, of these only fencing was considered of indispensable importance to the military mind, and it was implemented soon after the Academy was established.

The next suggestion of dancing instruction did not occur until 1815, and then it was not favorably received. Captain Alden Partridge, then Superintendent of the Academy, frowned on dancing and went so far as to issue an order forbidding "any petty parties or dances as they are injurious to the Institution," adding that the "cadets will find as much as they can do by properly attending to their studies and duties."

Two years later, Pierre Thomas, the Academy's first Swordmaster, was permitted by the Superintendent to organize a voluntary dancing class. These classes, initiated at the request of the cadets, were continued until 1823, when dancing was made compulsory for Third and Fourth Class cadets. According to the *Centennial History of the U.S. Military Academy*, a famous dance master named Papanti, from Boston, Massachusetts, was employed to instruct the cadets for three-quarters of an hour during their summer encampments. Reminiscenses of Professor Albert E. Church indicate that during his cadetship there were no formal dances, except those that were improvised by the cadets themselves, and those were generally country dances. "We had our regular dancing lessons. Our master for the whole four years was Papanti, the celebrated dancing master of Boston for nearly a half a century. He was not called "Professor" in those days. His wife was a famous singer, and often gave concerts in the chapel. Here she first sang to us the tunes now classic at graduation parades — "The Dashing White Sergeant," and "I See Them On Their Winding Way." She occasionally joined in our dancing lessons, much to our enjoyment, and during my cadetship, I think she was the only lady, with a single exception, who ever joined us in a dance at any time. This exception happened one evening of bright moonlight, in one of the country dances, when an officer, accompanied by a beautiful young lady from Albany, took his place at the dance. The fact became instantly known in camp, and cadets from all the companies, joining at the foot, extended the line to the guard-tent. She bravely went through the whole 'ere she could get out of the scrape."

In 1824, Eliza Leslie, sister of the distinguished English painter, Charles Leslie, wrote a letter to a friend from West Point. In it she described her experiences at dances at the Academy. She related how she had had several invitations to balls, but had only had an opportunity to accept two. The first was the dance given at the home of one of the professors. The second, given by the Corps of Cadets and held in the Mess Hall, impressed her greatly. She informed her friend how beautifully the hall was decorated for the occasion. The windows were shaded with laurel branches so arranged as to make each window look like an arbour or alcove. The pillars that supported the room were encircled with muskets and bayonets. Two elegant standards presented to the cadets by the citizens of Boston were suspended between the pillars. Miss Leslie added that the officers and cadets dressed in their uniforms added much to the animation of the scene. Her letter noted that the room was lighted with the same sconces that were used at the splendid ball given by the American officers to the French in honor of the birth of the Dauphin, when our Revolutionary Army was encamped at West Point.

The cadets appeared to have rather mixed feelings about dancing, which was rather natural for the times. For example, one cadet remarked in 1832 that "it was rather a dry business dancing without ladies; however, we cannot complain for the want of them in the evening. The cholera in New York had driven legions of girls here who generally, if they are not true orthodox, attend our cotillion parties very willingly."

An examination of the rich collection of memorabilia in the UMSA Library produced several early invitations to cadet "hops" or dances. One in particular is worthy of mention because it was sent to a female acquaintance of the then Cadet William T. Sherman in August, 1837. Cadet Sherman later became a brilliant Union Commander during the Civil War.

The famous Papanti's services were terminated in 1839 because more favorable terms were offered by another teacher of dance, one John Nevere. Based on the number of applications for the position, interest in dancing was apparently on the increase in America. Other candidates who applied for the vacancy at the time of Nevere's appointment were A. Bonand, L.J. Lucas, F.C. Labbe, and Lewis Carusi, all well-known instructors.

Another indication that dancing was becoming more popular at West Point and throughout the country was the increased attention given the subject in the newspapers. A cadet named William Dutton wrote a descriptive letter to his cousin on February 18, 1843 chiding the news editors of that day. A passage of the letter read as follows: "Many a time I have seen the "Guard turned out" & some man being missed — find him snoring on the ground without a blanket just like a hog — But our duties are so arduous together with walking one hour in 3 for the 24 — that exhaustion is the result. All I want of those editors who say that 'the lily fingered cadets, lounge in their velvet lawns — attend their brilliant balls & take pay for it,' as I saw in a paper yesterday — is that they may go through but one Plebe Encampment —." Despite such poor publicity from many of the newspapers and magazines of the day, there were others who wrote about and illustrated the fancy balls which were being held in Europe and the principal cities of the United States, including those held at West Point.

Prior to the Civil War a highly competent dancing master was hired at the Military Academy. His name was Edward Ferrero. Ferrero, of Italian parentage, was born in Granada, Spain on January 18, 1831. His father decided to move the family to New York City when Edward was only a young boy. The father had become a renowned dancing instructor and his talent rubbed off on his son. Under the elder man's watchful eye young Ferrero followed in his father's footsteps and became very successful. He was offered and quickly accepted the position of dancing master at West Point. His interests and expertise in dancing enabled him to author a volume entitled *The Art Of Dancing*, published in New York City in 1859. Unfortunately, his successful career at the Academy was short-lived because of the impending Civil War. Mustered into the services as a colonel of the 51st New York Infantry, Ferrero's record as a military officer was especially phenomenal and resulted in rapid promotion. He commanded a brigade at the second battle of Bull Run and also saw service at Chantilly, South Mountain, Antietam, and Fredericksburg. His appointment as a brigadier general was delivered to him on the battlefield of Antietam. Ultimately his lack of real knowledge of miliary tactics and strategy resulted in his downfall in the Union Army. His military career ended at

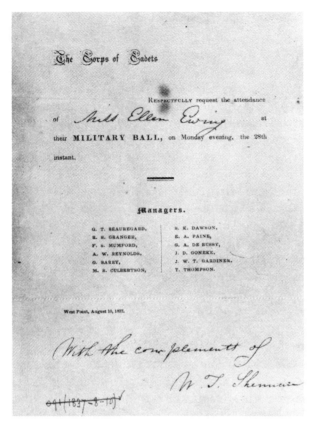

The Corps of Cadets

RESPECTFULLY request the attendance

of *Miss Ellen Ewing* at

their **MILITARY BALL**, on Monday evening, the 28th

instant.

Managers.

G. T. BEAUREGARD,	S. K. DAWSON,
R. S. GRANGER,	E. A. PAINE,
F. S. MUMFORD,	G. A. DE RUSSY,
A. W. REYNOLDS,	J. D. GONEKE,
G. BARRY,	J. W. T. GARDINER,
M. S. CULBERTSON,	T. THOMPSON.

West Point, August 10, 1837.

With the complements of

W. T. Sherman

Invitation to a Military Ball, dated August 10, 1837, and sent to Miss Ellen Ewing by Cadet William T. Sherman. Miss Ewing latter married General Sherman.

A Cadet Hop at West Point, c1859

the conclusion of the war and, after regaining civilian status, he once again returned to New York City.

The popularity of dancing at the Military Academy during the 1850s and particularly the feelings of the cadets towards it is easily documented. However, during and for some time after the Civil War instruction in the art of dancing was in a state of limbo at the Academy. It was curtailed during the War because of the accelerated curriculum required to graduate more officers for active duty in the field. The records for the period are rather scanty; they do show, however, that in the early 1870s the dancing master was a Mr. H. Hlasko who resided at the Rossmore Hotel in New York City. Hlasko remained in the position through the summer of 1878, but in the spring of 1879 he asked the Superintendent to relieve him from his duties so that he could go abroad to France. Superintendent John M. Schofield approved his request and filled the vacancy by appointing Mr. Louis W. Vizay to the position. Thus began the tenure of one of the greatest father and son teams in West Point history. In 1883, Professor Vizay was joined at the Academy by his son, Rudolph, who was subsequently employed as his father's assistant. Both men were truly dedicated in their service to the Corps of Cadets. Professor Louis Vizay remained as the dancing master through the summer of 1898 when he tendered his resignation. Superintendent Albert L. Mills expressed his appreciation to Professor Vizay for his services by stating that "no higher encomium could be placed upon your services than the fact that you have served under different Superintendents for nineteen consecutive years with perfect satisfaction." It was only fitting that Professor Vizay's son should be appointed to fill the vacancy. He had been tutored well by his father, and he accepted the responsibilities with the same dedication and loyalty.

Since the Military Academy was and still is an institution devoted to turning out not only capable Army officers but also polished gentlemen, "dancing and ballroom etiquette" was of primary concern to the Vizays. During the early 1900s dancing instruction was of considerable importance to the cadets. The instruction given by Professor Vizay was regarded by them as another part of their curriculum which would be beneficial throughout the remainder of their lives. Cadets approached the

Professor Rudolph W. Vizay, Dance Instructor

lessons with the same spirited attitude with which they approached any other military drill. Regimentation during this period was much more strict than it is today; dancing lessons were formed in ranks, and the cadets marched to and from the lessons.

Rudolph Vizay maintained excellent control over the conduct of his classes. He was given the utmost respect, and the cadets obeyed his directions as though they were commands of a military officer. Initially, the cadets were taught the part of the gentleman, or "lead," in dancing, and then the part of the lady. This method enabled them to dance with each other, and they took alternate parts each day.

The younger Vizay's career as instructor and dancing master at West Point spanned a total of fifty-two years. As a tribute to his faithful services a former Commandant of Cadets once wrote him and remarked that "your association with West Point has been one of the most potent influences for good and you have contributed not only to the discipline of the Corps of Cadets, but your usually fine instruction in dancing has aided in creating the rhythmic beauty of their marching, which is so universally recognized."

Professor Rudolph Vizay expressed his viewpoints on modern dancing just four years prior to his death in 1935. In 1931, while serving as President of the American Society of Teachers of Dancing, he addressed the convention in New York City. Vizay made it a point to stress how unfortunate it was that public taste in the art of dancing was changing. He elaborated upon the beauty of the polkas, lancers, and mazurkas of yesteryear and then proceeded to comment and casually complain about the easygoing manners of the 1930's. He then proceeded as follows: "Why, a young man does not even know enough to get up when a girl comes to speak to him and he dances all night with the one girl; in fact, she will not permit him to dance with anyone else. In the old days it was always the first and the last, while the girl filled up her program in between. We are trying to restore etiquette to the dance, a little dignity, a little formality, an occasional bow, instead of a rough grab for one's partner." Unfortunately, the rapid pace of our changing times had affected dancing as much and probably more than any of our other cultural traditions of past generations.

The pleasure of your presence is requested AT THE

FAREWELL HOP

Given to the

Graduating Class

OF THE

United States Military Academy,

WEST POINT,

THURSDAY EVENING JUNE 12 1884.

MANAGERS

JOHN C W BROOKS   HAYDN S COLE   JOHN LITTLE
FRANK DeW RAMSEY   EDWARD R GILMAN   WM E CRAIGHILL
PHILIP A BETTENS   CORNELIS DeW WILLCOX   BEAUMONT B BUCK

German Leaders

WALDO E AYER.   SAM'L D STURGIS, Jr.

Invitation to the Graduation Hop, Class of 1884.

Professor Vizay died at the West Point Hospital on March 1, 1935, at the age of 77. His passing ended an era of fifty-six years in which dancing enjoyed immense popularity at the United States Military Academy. From the initial employment of the celebrated Papanti in 1823, West Point has witnessed many distinguished dancing masters. None, however, had the personal impact or contributed more to the history of Academy dance than Louis and Rudolph Vizay!

Despite the lack of an official dancing master on the staff, instruction did not end with the death of Professor Vizay in 1935. The Commandant of Cadets appointed a board of officers to make recommendations for a suitable replacement. After screening applicants the board recommended that Mr. and Mrs. George H. Roberts of Tulsa, Oklahoma be employed as dancing instructors. Their services were terminated in 1941 because of the World War II emergency. The dancing course was eliminated as a required part of cadet instruction.

In 1943, Miss Barbara F. Cation began instructing the cadets in dancing on a voluntary basis. She had an excellent background in dancing and remained at the Academy and performed in an exemplary manner through 1948. The instruction from that period has been more or less on a voluntary basis and the instructors were most admirable. One in particular is certainly worthy of mention in this article. Mr. William Lewis, presently an academy physical education instructor, has been a noted ballroom dancer and square dance caller for over a quarter of a century at West Point. During the early 1950s when dancing appeared to be in the process of waning, Mr. Lewis capably took charge and instructed the cadets in the fox trot, polka, cha cha, jitterbug, and most importantly, the waltz. He made sure that every cadet could glide gracefully over the floor to the tune of "Army Blue," the closing number of each cadet hop.

With individuals of Mr. Lewis' caliber, the authorities at West Point can rest assured that the art of dancing implemented during the early history of the Military Academy will continue for many more years to come.

HUCKLEBERRY FINN
VISITS
WEST POINT

Samuel L. Clemens, the great humorist and novelist, better known by the pseudonym "Mark Twain," was a frequent visitor to the Military Academy between the years 1880 and 1906.

In 1887 an announcement was made to the cadets and all post personnel that Mark Twain would deliver a lecture in the Cadet Mess Hall on 30 April 1887. The subject of Twain's lecture for the evening was entitled "English as She is Taught." It consisted of questions and humorous answers given by students. Some of the subjects discussed were: Grammar, Mathematics, Geography, History, Philosophy, Astronomy, and Music.

Mark Twain cited some of the children's quaint definitions of words and showed how the children were misled by the sound of the word, or by the observation of it on paper. Twain's examples were as follows:

Alias — a good man in the Bible.
Amenable — anything that is mean.
Emolument — a headstone to a grave.
Equestrian — one who asks questions.
Franchise — anything belonging to the French.
Irrigate — to make fun of.
Mercenary — one who feels for another.
Parasite — a kind of umbrella.

In the subject of Mathematics, Twain gave the following examples:

A straight line is any distance between two places.

Parallel lines are lines that can never meet until they run together.

To find the number of square feet in a room you multiply the room by the number of the feet. The product is the result.

To conclude his lecture, Twain recited the following composition written by a boy on the subject of girls:

ON GIRLS

Girls are very stuckup and dignefied in their maner and be have your. They think more of dress than anything else and like to play with dowls and rags. They cry if they see a cow in a far distance and are afraid of guns. They stay at home all the time and go to church on Sunday. They are al-ways sick. They are al-ways funy and making fun of boy's hands and they say how dirty. They cant play marbels. I pity them poor things. They make fun of boys and then turn round and love them. I dont beleave they ever kiled a cat or anything. They look out every nite and say oh ant the moon lovely. Thir is one thing I have not told and that is they al-ways now their lessons bettern boys.

To give you an idea how the cadets and the personnel of West Point enjoyed Mr. Twain's lecture and humor, a summary of the event as extracted from the *Army and Navy Journal*, Volume 23, (May 1887), page 815, follows:

On Saturday evening the Cadet Mess Hall was thrown open for the first time since it has received its new and handsome decorations. Exclamations of surprise and pleasure greeted these changes, which are certainly fine. An unusually large and brilliant audience welcomed with a storm of applause the arrival of "Mark Twain." He entered the room with Professor Postlethwait and was escorted to the platform. The reading this time was on the article that appeared in the April "Century," "English as She is Taught" — which aroused simply roars of laughter, but the cream of the fun was the remark, "There were donkeys in the Theological Seminary," and his immediately turning round to explain to the chaplain that nothing personal was intended, was so indescribably funny that the audience continued to laugh and applaud for fully five minutes.

On Saturday afternoon the Corps of Cadets was reviewed by General Merritt. Mr. Clemens was invited to accompany the reviewing party. He committed a court-martial offence by forgetting to throw away his cigar before taking his place in line with the staff.

General Wesley Merritt, Superintendent, U.S. Military Academy, 1882-1887. General Merritt, a close friend of Mark Twain, was instrumental in arranging the latter's visits.

To emphasize the close relationship that existed between West Point and Mark Twain, a letter discovered in the USMA Archives reveals that on February 28, 1906, the superintendent wrote to Mr. Samuel Clemens to acknowledge the receipt of a beautiful photograph he had sent of himself. A portion of this letter written by the superintendent relates the following:

For the Academy and all connected with it I thank you for this testimony of your regard, and I venture to hope when the spring blossoms are fully out and it is more comfortable to move about than at present, you may feel inclined to again honor West Point with a visit. I believe you will find much here to interest and entertain you in the changes that have taken place and are under way, and I certainly can assure you a hearty welcome from many friends who recollect and often speak of your former pleasant visits.

A careful search of archival material failed to indicate any further reference to Mark Twain visiting the Military Academy after the exchange of correspondence in 1906.

It is interesting to note that Mark Twain's book entitled *Mark Twain's (Date, 1601), Conversation as it Was by the Social Fireside in the Time of the Tudors*, was first printed on the West Point press. Twain visited his close friend, Lieutenant C.E.S. Wood, who was the adjutant at the Military Academy in 1881, and learned that Wood supervised a small printing establishment on the post. After Twain returned to Connecticut, he sent a letter to Lieutenant Wood asking if he would consider printing something he had written, which he felt should not be entrusted to a commercial printer. Lieutenant Wood responded that he would be glad to oblige, hence the first printing of Twain's book was completed at West Point. The volume contains a bit of Mr. Twain's salty Elizabethan dialogue.

The State of Missouri has endeared itself to generations of Americans through the writing of Mark Twain. A fine example of this was revealed in a letter written by a Mr. Williston Fish, a graduate of the Class of 1881. The letter, dated August 26, 1900, and addressed to Samuel L. Clemens in London, England, clearly documents the sharp impact that Twain had on the readers of his many works.

The excerpt from the letter reads as follows:

The world would not have been the same world without you. Mark Twain is just like the sun and the skies and the apple-orchards. His books are just the same as living. All good people would like to do something to give you pleasure, such as you give the rest of us, but I don't know how we can do it unless we send you a set of your own works.

The great American humorist died in 1910, and his death caused a more universal regret than has ever followed the death of any other American man of letters.

ROCK-BOUND PATRIOTISM
Richard Delafield and The Stone Inscriptions

During the year 1857 Major Richard Delafield, then serving his second tour of duty as superintendent of the United States Military Academy, had an unusual idea which has had a lasting impression on the United States Corps of Cadets. Strangely enough, his idea has had greater historical significance during our country's recent Bicentennial Year than it did for the first one hundred and eighteen years.

Delafield was an extremely patriotic individual, and his interest in American history was clearly exemplified when he directed that the names of three major Revolutionary War battles be inscribed on rock ledges in various locations on the West Point Reservation. His intention was to insure that lasting memorials of our country's heritage would leave an impression on the minds of young cadets in the future. Unfortunately, the written records concerning this patriotic act are rather scanty. The only information available in the United States Military Academy Archives which verifies that Delafield was responsible for the accomplishment is a letter dated 26 April 1912 from William Ward, who had been the chief clerk in the adjutant's office for nearly a half century. Ward's letter was in response to a memorandum he had received from his successor, requesting information about who had directed the names of certain Revolutionary battles to be cut into the rocks. His quick and informative reply stated that "as near as I can remember (at this distant day) the names were cut by direction of Major Delafield, during his second administration, probably about 1857 or 8."

The names of the battles inscribed on the granite ledges were *Bunker Hill, Saratoga,* and *Yorktown.* The only other pertinent information available is contained in the early treasurer's records which reveal that on three separate dates the total sum of $109.60 was paid to one Peter Fritz as a fee for lettering the stone.

The Bunker Hill inscription was cut into a rock ledge along the river, just west of the present railroad tracks. It was removed shortly after 1920 during the process of widening the road for the newly constructed West Shore Railroad stationhouse. Although the authorities were reluctant to remove the inscription, they felt it advisable to do so, reasoning that West Point was quickly becoming a great attraction to the public and that adequate transportation facilities had to be provided.

The rock ledge with the Saratoga inscription is appropriately located adjacent to Kosciuszko's Garden at the start of the well-known "Flirtation Walk." This inscription, because of its more convenient location, has been viewed more frequently by cadets, post personnel, and visitors than either of the other two inscriptions. Last spring I decided to take a leisurely stroll and ended up at the Kosciuszko Garden site. No other soul was in the quiet and especially peaceful surroundings, and I felt great pride when I realized that I was standing on the same spot the famous Revolutionary hero had visited on numerous occasions. The beautiful flowers and shrubs had reached their peak, and the entire scene was simply breathtaking. There were at least twenty varieties of flowers. The multi-colored tulips stood like cadets at a parade formation. The fully bloomed azalea bushes were dazzling in beauty, and the ferns in the background created one of the most picturesque views I have ever witnessed. Just beyond stands the massive rock ledge with the indelible inscription reading "Saratoga, 17th October 1777." The brass plaque near the base of the ledge states: "Kosciuszko's Garden — Built in 1778 for rest and meditation by the brilliant Polish military engineer who redesigned and supervised construction of the forts at West Point making it the 'Gibraltar of the Hudson' in the Revolution." There was no question in my mind that Major Delafield's selection of this magnificent site for the inscription of *Saratoga* was indeed an appropriate one.

I next visited the area of the Yorktown inscription, located farther north along Flirtation Walk on the prominent ledge facing Constitution Island. The lilacs were in bloom and their fragrance was every where. The large bold letters YORKTOWN

Major Richard Delafield, Superintendent, 1838-1845, 1856-
1861.

Bunker Hill inscription, originally located behind the railroad station and
removed in the 1920s.

appeared literally to reach out and seize my attention. While enjoying the unforgettable handiwork of mother nature the only noises I heard were the singing of birds and a distant train whistle from across the river.

It is worthwhile to mention a few significant facts concerning Richard Delafield's background and sterling character; they probably inspired him to have the names of the memorable battles cut into the ledges. His father, John Delafield, emigrated to the United States from Europe in 1783 and settled in New York City. He became so successful as a merchant that he was later referred to as "one of the fathers of Wall Street."

Richard Delafield was admitted to the United States Military Academy on 4 May 1814, at the age of 15 years, 10 months. He graduated at the head of his class on 24 July 1818, and holds the distinction of being the first cadet to whom an "order of merit" was assigned. This was one of Sylvanus Thayer's innovations, and from that day class rank has been one of the distinguishing features at the Academy, inspiring cadets to strive for academic and military excellence. The "order of merit" was discontinued with the Class of 1978.

Following graduation, Delafield spent the next twenty years on various engineering projects for the Corps of Engineers. His superiors noted that in the course of his duties he showed a marked ability to handle executive matters. When the vacancy for the superintendency of the Military Academy arose in 1838, Delafield was selected for the coveted position. His contributions were many, and their effect on the physical plant of West Point and the Corps of Cadets are still evident to the present day. One of his first objectives was the overall improvement of the post itself. He was instrumental in seeing that new roads were built, and that badly needed new living quarters were constructed for the comfort of post personnel. Another particularly interesting Delafield accomplishment was the well-designed and beautiful "Chain Battery Walk." Over the years its name had been changed by the cadets to the familiarly known "Flirtation Walk." The romantic site, which winds its way alongside the majestic Hudson River, received national recognition in 1934 after the filming of the Hollywood movie bearing the same name.

An examination of Richard Delafield's superintendency reveals that he was not particularly liked by the cadets, although they certainly respected him for his ability and leadership qualities. They knew him as a strict disciplinarian who ruled with an "iron hand." As the years passed and these same cadets became more mature with age and experience, their personal feelings towards him changed. They realized hs was a strong leader who wanted to insure that they learned their lessons well and were properly trained in the art of warfare. To prove this point, the following letter of condolence written by a former cadet was received by Mrs. Delafield after the General's death:

Headquarters, Army of
the United States
Washington, D.C.,
Nov. 5, 1873

Mrs. General Delafield
Washington, D.C.

Dear Madam:

Pardon me for intruding at this moment of supreme sorrow. The President and I have arranged to attend a Fair at Leesburgh tomorrow, and I will go over and see him, so that he may decide what he will do. I will not go in any event, but remain here to do whatever I can to manifest my love, respect, and affection for General Delafield.

Were it my office, it would be a labor of love for me to prepare his obituary order, but this will devolve on the Secretary of War, as the Engineer Corps is not construed as a part of my military family. In the future do look to me as the friend of your family, and command my services whenever I can do or say anything to commemorate the virtues of one that, I think, I appreciated from the moment he became Superintendent of the Military Academy, when I was a mere boy. I then, by a mere chance, learned that beneath his severe exterior was a warm sympathetic heart for those entrusted to his care.

Sympathizing deeply in your bereavement.

I am, with sincere respect,

Your friend and servant,
W.T. SHERMAN, General

Unfortunately, and as happens so frequently, General Delafield never really received the full recognition that should have been accorded to him. Perhaps it was because he was not one to publicize or boast of his many accomplishments. A letter written by him at the twilight of his military career was recently uncovered; it explains his personal feelings concerning self adulation. The letter was addressed to Captain George W. Cullum, who was seeking information from former graduates while preparing his monumental *Biographical Register Of The Officers and Graduates Of The U.S. Military Academy.* Prior to furnishing Cullum with a brief summary of his military service, Delafield remarked, "I do confess my unwillingness to write anything about self for public reading. I have got so far in life that quiet and rest, rather than work, toil and labor, are more covetous than the reverse and hence no longer am ambitious of holding myself up from previous labors and experience as suited particularly for anything—."

At one time or another we have probably all heard friends or neighbors comment during a Fourth of July observance that they were proud to be Americans. General Delafield was also proud, but, he additionally had enough foresight and patriotism to insure that our country's heritage would not be soon forgotten. He was a true and loyal American!

As a final note on patriotism and rock carvings at the Academy, the reader should know that a few Mexican War events are also commemorated in stone near the northern vicinity of Flirtation Walk. This was done in 1847 during the superintendency of Henry Brewerton. Near the conclusion of the war, Brewerton published an order dated 14 April 1847 announcing to the Corps of Cadets the brilliant victories achieved by the United States Forces in Mexico. He cited two graduates, William R. McKee, Class of 1829, and Henry Clay, Class of 1831, who had been killed in action at Buena Vista. Colonel Clay was the son of the great orator and statesman. Brewerton concluded the order by stating that "while we mourn the loss of these our companions in arms, they serve as bright examples for our imitation, and I can perform no more fitting duty on this occasion, than to point to the gallant acts of these your predecessors at the Institution, and to ask you to emulate them in deeds of valor should fortune ever lead you to the battlefield."

A short time after the publication of Brewerton's order, Mr. Samuel D. Flagg was hired as the stonecutter to inscribe the names of the prominent Mexican War events on stone. These include *Palo Alto, Reseca De La Palma,* and *Vera Cruz.* Flagg's total compensation for the services rendered was $166.22, in all probability the going rate of pay for stonecutters of the period.

Generals Delafield and Brewerton should be remembered for their patriotic deeds. Both graduates expressed their deepest love and admiration for their country in a truly fitting manner. They were excellent examples of United States Military Academy products, and both found a proper method of expressing their feelings. With such a tribute to the heritage of the United States it is apparent that both men also lived up to the well-known motto of their Alma Mater: "DUTY, HONOR, COUNTRY."

HAUGHTY BILL

The Army Officer Who Instilled The High Standards
Of Military Bearing and Drill Precision in The
U.S. Corps Of Cadets

Everyone, young or old, enjoys the thrilling experience of witnessing a grand parade, with the blare of bugles and the ruffle of drums and the American Flag waving proudly, to remind us of our glorious history.

To a great number of people it is always a welcomed sight to see the U.S. Corps of Cadets participating in these military displays. The precision of their various marching maneuvers is known throughout the world. West Point and its cadets' participation in parades have a particular association with the American Flag. It is the oldest U.S. Military post in continuous occupation, having first been garrisoned by American troops in 1778.

Let's look back through the Military Academy's history to determine who was responsible for instilling these soldierly characteristics in the cadets.

When Sylvanus Thayer assumed the superintendency of the Academy in 1817 he appointed an officer of the Army to serve as the instructor of infantry tactics and soldierly discipline. It was not until 1825, however, that the position of Commandant of Cadets was established by USMA Regulations, and it was not until 12 June 1858 that Congress first recognized the title of Commandant of Cadets. In March 1820, Thayer selected Major William J. Worth to fill the vacancy created by the transfer of Captain John R. Bell, a graduate of the Class of 1812. It is surprising to note that Major Worth was not a West Pointer. After obtaining a common school education at Hudson, New York, he applied for a commission in the U.S. Army and was appointed a first lieutenant during the War of 1812. He reached the rank of brevet major by the end of the war. As the aide-de-camp to General Winfield Scott, Worth fought gallantly at the battles of Chippewa and Lundy's Lane. In the latter battle he was so severely wounded that it was felt he would die. After being confined to bed for nearly a year, and realizing he would be lamed for life, he still remained in the Army.

Major Worth was above average height, an erect, well-built man, with dark hair and very dark eyes, which might almost be said to be black; these and his compressed lips gave his face the expression of determination that was peculiarly remarkable. Prior to Worth's assignment as commandant, the cadets obeyed Captains Bliss and Bell merely because they were their officers but when Major Worth took command they obeyed him because he made them a part, as it were, of himself. There was something magnetic in his voice and manner that seemed to establish a close relationship between the cadets and their commandant when on drill. It is to Major Worth, in great measure, that the cadets, even those of today, are indebted for their soldierly qualities.

The following account of the Corps of Cadets march to Boston, Massachusetts during the summer of 1821 was published in the Springfield newspaper *Hampden Patriot and Liberal Recorder*. It emphasizes Major Worth's superlative leadership qualities in administering the cadets of West Point.

THE CADETS

Wednesday, August 1, 1821. — This interesting corps of youthful soldiers left the Academy at West Point, under the command of Maj. Worth, on the 20th ult. on a tour of exercise, instruction and observation, — reached Albany in steamboats on the morning of the 21st, where they were honored by every possible attention of the citizens, and of the authorities, civil and military, during their stay in that city. On the morning of the 24th, between 5 and 6, they left Albany on their march eastward, passing through Lebanon; they reached Westfield on Saturday 28th, where they encamped for the night, and arrived at this place early Sunday morning — pitched their tents on the enclosure in front of the U.S. Armory — attended public worship at the Episcopal Chapel, and remained at this encampment when our paper went to press. We understand they were to take up their line of march this morning for the eastward. They are to pass

Major William J. Worth, Commandant of Cadets, 1820-1828.

through Worcester for Boston, where arrangements have been made to give them a most splendid reception. They are to return to West Point by the way of Providence, New London and New Haven. We are thus particular in tracing their course, from the persuasion that our readers will consider no incident too trifling to mention, which relates to this expedition of a band of military pupils to whom all eyes are directed. It needs scarcely be added, that the citizens of Springfield and its vicinity were highly gratified by their manly and soldier-like deportment; indeed, the admiration manifest in the countenance of every beholder, seemed heightened into astonishment at the wonderful exactness of their movements on parade; and one gentleman observed, "they seemed like one entire and connected machine, moving simultaneously, as it were, by the act of touching a wire!" The charm of this exhibition was not a little heightened by the performances of the band of music attached to the corps, said to be the best in the United States. The whole corps consists of 250, which is the maximum number fixed by law. There are present in this expedition 210 cadets, exclusive of their officers, viz: Major W.J. Worth, who is the instructor of tactics at the Academy; Lt. H.W. Griswold, and Lt. Z.J.D. Kinsley, assistant instructors of tactics. Major Worth served throughout the late war, with great credit to himself, and was distinguished for his skill and bravery in the battles of Chippewa and Bridgewater. The Academy at West Point is under the superintendence of Major Sylvanus Thayer, of the Corps of Engineers, and has several able professors & teachers of natural and experimental philosophy, of mathematics, engineering, ethics, tactics, chemistry and mineralogy, french, and drawing, which are all the branches there taught. No cadets are admitted except between the age of 14 and 21. They are divided into 4 classes, and their term of instruction is 4 years, although they engage to serve a year longer if required. The graduates are entitled to commissions in the Army, and are obliged to accept them when offered. Their discipline while at the Academy, is extremely rigid. Ten months in the year are devoted to their studies, two of which are exclusively devoted to the study of tactics. They are excluded from all society except that of the Corps. As evidence of the rigid discipline and requirements, we perceive by the Register of the Officers and Cadets, politely furnished us by Major Worth, that out of 210 cadets who were examined at the general examination in June last, 43 were found deficient, and turned back to re-commence the studies of their respective classes. The pay of the cadets is 16 dollars per month and two rations, equal in all to 28 dollars.

We should not omit to mention, that one object of their excursion is to make such topographical observation as may be of use hereafter in the event of a war; Mr. Prescott, one of the cadets, went on Monday, to the foot of Mount Holyoke, for the purpose of ascertaining its elevation. We

Review of Corps of Cadets on the occasion of the Hudson-Fulton Celebration, 1909. German Kaiser Wilhelm inscribed the photograph: "A fine body of promising young gentlemen! A sight delightful to a soldier's heart!"

Cadets on Parade, with Cadet Chapel in the background.

had not heard the result when our paper went to press. It has heretofore been estimated at about 1200 feet above the level of the Connecticut River, which washes its base.

Since the above was in type, we are informed that in addition to the commissioned officers above named, Lieutenant Tompkins, of the corps of Ordnance, who is a nephew of the Vice President, is attached to the corps of Cadets, and is now with them, acting as Quarter Master.

The statement in the foregoing account that reads "they [the Corps of Cadets] seemed like one entire and connected machine, moving simultaneously, as it were, by the act of touching a wire," was a tremendous compliment to Major Worth, since the Corps's success was a tribute to his leadership.

It can truthfully be said that Major William J. Worth left a mark upon the Corps of Cadets that has never been effaced.

Although this distinguished soldier received the rank of brevet major general for his gallant and meritorious conduct in the Mexican War, he never received the proper accolades he so rightfully deserved. As a matter of fact, there is a monument erected in his honor on Fifth Avenue in New York City, but of the thousands of people who pass by it daily, only a few have the slightest idea who General Worth was or have any knowledge of his tremendous accomplishments in the military profession.

General Worth does hold the distinction of having two American cities named in his honor, Fort Worth, Texas, and Lake Worth, Florida; however, this is a meager reward when one considers his valuable contributions to the U.S. Army and to his country.

EDWARD SINGLETON HOLDEN
Astronomer and Librarian

In another century we may perhaps be willing to boast of our results. Even now, we have every reason to feel confidence in the future since the performance of the past has not been unworthy of our opportunity. (Professor E.S. Holden, commenting on America's achievements in space science, *Forum*, August 1893.)

Over a century ago a graduate named Captain George H. Derby, Class of 1846, made the following humorous remark concerning the moon: "As to the moon, we are told that if anyone from our planet succeeds in reaching it, it will probably be a woman, as the sex will never cease making an exertion for that purpose as long as there is a man in it."

Man's dream of traveling to the moon and possibly to other planets has become a reality in our lifetime. Through the magnificent efforts and achievements of our scientists and astronomers it has been possible for our courageous astronauts to travel in their space vehicles, and to reach their goals with precision and accuracy.

The contributions of the Military Academy and its graduates toward America's achievements in astronomy can be recorded from the time of the institution's establishment in 1802. In that year the United States Military Philosophical Society was founded by Colonel Jonathan Williams, the first Academy superintendent and the grandnephew of Benjamin Franklin. Williams stated in one of the Society's early meetings that "military science is in its own nature so diffuse, that it is almost impossible to designate any dividing lines. Astronomy, geography, and mathematics run into each other at every step."

Professor Ferdinand R. Hassler, a native of Switzerland, emigrated to the United States in 1807 to accept a position of Professor of Mathematics at the Academy. He served in this capacity for approximately two years and resigned when he was selected by President Thomas Jefferson to be the first director of the United States Coast Survey. He was the able head of that Department until his death in 1843. His sincere dedication and unquestioned scientific ability was recognized by his peers in the profession at that time.

Alexander D. Bache, Class of 1825, succeeded Professor Hassler and was regarded by renowned scientists as the true father of the U.S. Coast and Geodetic Survey Department. He furthered the efforts of Professor Hassler by devising instruments and methods which stimulated the interests of his staff for future scientific experimentation.

Ormsby M. Mitchel, Class of 1829, created the widespread popular interest in astronomy in America by presenting famous lectures which lead to the foundation of many private and college observatories in our nation.

One of the foremost astronomers in our nation's history was an Academy graduate who was born just ten years prior to Captain Derby's whimsical comment. Edward S. Holden was born November 5, 1846 in St. Louis, Missouri. His mother died of cholera when he was three, and the boy was sent to Cambridge, Massachusetts where he was cared for by his father's sister. His early education was received from his cousin who had at the time an excellent school in Cambridge. Furthermore, the cousin's sister was married to the director of the Harvard College Observatory, and young Holden benefited from the latter's diversified knowledge of astronomy.

Holden entered Washington University at St. Louis in 1863, and it was not long before his fine qualities and vast knowledge were recognized by Professor William Chauvenet, the accomplished mathematician, astronomer, and chancellor of the university. Holden studied under the professor's watchful eye, and a year later Chauvenet, when on convalescent sick leave in Minnesota, wished Holden to accompany him. Chauvenet became so impressed by Holden's personality and aptitude that he disliked the idea of parting from his pupil!

Cadet Edward S. Holden, Class of 1870.

Professor Edward S. Holden, Librarian, U.S. Military Academy, 1902-1914.

Holden later returned to college and graduated in June 1866 with a bachelor of science degree. He was forever mindful and grateful to Professor Chauvenet for influencing him to enter the field of astronomy. However, as strange as it may seem, he received a congressional appointment to West Point and entered in September 1866. He found academics to be relatively easy because of his previous background in the mathematical sciences. For this reason he was able to spend much of his leisure time visiting and reading in the Academy's library. His association with certain professors was unique and was shared by only a few other cadets at that time.

Cadet Holden graduated from the Academy on June 15, 1870, standing number three in a class of 58 members and was commissioned in the Fourth Artillery. The following year he was ordered back to West Point to serve as assistant professor of natural and experimental philosophy. After a successful two year tour at the Academy he resigned from the Army to accept a position at the Washington Naval Observatory. It was because of his devotion and love for astronomy that Holden decided to leave the Army. For the next twenty-five years his chief interests lay in the sciences; however, the writer of a short biographical piece would be foolish to attempt to go into detail concerning his scientific writings and achievements. For the astronomy buffs a complete listing of his writings can be found in the second volume of the *Centennial History of the United States Military Academy.*

In that twenty-five year period Professor Holden held such prominent positions as director of the Washburn Observatory at the University of Wisconsin, president of the University of California and director of the famous Lick Observatory in California. It was noted by one of Holden's fellow astronomers after the former's departure as director that "the evidence of Professor Holden's organizing ability and energy are written all over the Lick Observatory." He was also the founder of the Astronomical Society of the Pacific. Additionally, when time permitted, he devoted personal research in the photography of the moon which enabled him to write scholarly articles for *Harper's Weekly* and many noted scientific and engineering journals of the day.

Main Reading Room, U.S. Military Academy Library, c1914.

U.S. Military Academy Library, c1914. Dade Monument in foreground was later moved to the Post Cemetery.

Although Holden had severed relations with the Military Academy a few years after graduation, his thoughts of and interest in the school's welfare remained with him for the rest of his life. His close friendship and adminiration for another graduate led him to accept the position as the first full-time librarian in the history of the Military Academy.

Professor Samuel E. Tillman, head of the Department of Chemistry, was instrumental in convincing Holden to fill this responsible vacancy. Prior to Holden's appointment it had always been the custom for one of the professors to hold this honorary office, and it was attended to in spare moments. Tillman was of the definite opinion that the Academy needed an able full-time librarian and his thoughts on the matter were eventually concurred in by both the superintendent and the Board of Visitors.

Holden held to the doctrine that "the library is the principle of life of every institution of instruction, whose tone can never rise higher than the means for teaching its instructors." Using this concept, he devoted his entire efforts to insuring that the USMA Library would meet the needs of every instructor and cadet. He supported this theory by obtaining the most recent works available for each academic department. In addition, Holden believed that the USMA Library should make every effort to have closer relationships with all other acknowledged important libraries throughout the world. His chief contribution, however, was placing the library in proper relationship to the academic departments, cadets, officers, and dependents residing on the post. Holden's services at the Academy can be summed up by stating that his presence as librarian gave the library a prominence in the literary and scientific world that it had never before enjoyed.

Professor Holden possessed a wide variety of interests in life. He was an accomplished after dinner speaker (a friend once testified that his conversation was entertaining to the point of brilliancy!), and an examination of his personal papers in the custody of the Special Collections Division of the USMA Library verifies this. The papers contain several handwritten bound volumes titled "The Diner Out"; these contain miscellaneous anecdotes and humorous stories that Professor Holden told at dinner conversations over the years. One seems particularly appropriate because it ties in with his dedicated life in astronomy. The piece is titled "The Universe Careless of Man," and reads as follows:

A good old Baptist minister had come a long way to see the wonders of the Smithsonian Institution Museum. At the door he was shown a huge meteorite. "That weighs half a ton, did you say?" — "Things like that are revolving about in the sky and every now and then falling to the earth?" — "If one should strike a man, it would kill him, or if one should hit a church it would destroy the church and all the people" — "Well (with a sigh) I've always known that God was good — but I think He is mighty careless. (sic)

Probably the finest tribute that could have been paid to Professor Holden was contained in a letter written in 1915 by Dr. Talcott Williams, the first director and dean of the Columbia School of Journalism. Dr. Williams had been an associate and close acquaintance of distinguished Americans for over forty years. The letter was written to Professor Samuel E. Tillman, who two years later would serve as the superintendent of the Academy. The full text of the letter reads as follows:

My Dear Professor — I am profoundly indebted to you for the memorial of our dear friend Holden, which I have just received, having been away for two months in the West. It sums up the life of the most extraordinary man I have ever known. We have both known men more successful and more crowned with the world's honors, but, for myself, for sheer lambent intellect I have never known his equal. In those vivid days (1877) when I first knew him he had an influence on my life which has lasted to this day. Much of the work that I am now doing in the school springs from the directions in which he led my ideas and reading at that time. Again with appreciation for what you have written, I am, sincerely yours,

TALCOTT WILLIAMS

To date the Academy has contributed a number of astronauts who have ventured in space. The names of all will be recorded in history, and rightfully so; nevertheless, history should not overlook the brilliant graduate whose contributions in astronomy — specifically, his extensive telescopic exploration of the moon — helped make it possible for mankind to explore the entire universe.

CAPTAIN GEORGE H. DERBY
alias
JOHN PHOENIX

Every graduate of the U.S. Military Academy has witnessed the escapades of an honest-to-goodness practical joker. It is unfortunate, however, that the majority of West Pointers and the general public have never heard about the remarkable tales of the Corps's most notorious practical joker, George H. Derby, Class of 1846.

The graduating Class of 1846 contained on its roster such illustrious military leaders as Thomas J. (Stonewall) Jackson, George B. McClellan, and George E. Pickett who led the Confederate charge at Gettysburg.

Cadet Derby, however, made his mark in another field of endeavor, the literary profession; he was responsible for the development of the boisterous "Western" style of humor in our country. As a cadet, Derby established a reputation as a wit and notorious practical joker, and his reputation remained with him throughout the rest of his life. Here are a few examples of Derby's foolery and wit.

As a cadet Derby transformed all the pictures in his geology textbook of bones and fossils of the antediluvian periods into strange monsters. The regulations of the Military Academy naturally considered this a serious offense, and Derby's textbook on geology was seized and placed before the Academic Board, where it caused such irresistible laughter that the Board decided not to interview or punish the delinquent.

A second offense of a similar nature happened shortly thereafter. As a result of Cadet Derby's passion for illustrating textbooks the authorities saw fit to keep a watchful eye on the sly cadet. This merely proved to be more of a challenge to

Derby who seemed to thrive on "beating the system." The incident happened in the following manner:

Professor Theophile D'Oremieulx, an instructor in the French Department, had Derby and his classmates assembled for the daily French lesson. A brief moment after the instruction began, D'Oremieulx, hesitated and interrupting himself, remarked "Ah! it is the first of the month, I see. Gentlemen, hand me your textbooks." All the cadets in attendance quickly made a move to obey his instructions with the exception of Cadet Derby. He was observed hastily seizing his textbook and quickly attempting to hide it in his desk drawer.

"Mr. Derby," said Professor D'Oremieulx sternly, "hand me your textbook, sir."

"Could I be excused just this once, sir?" faltered Derby.

"Certainly not, sir" returned Professor D'Oremieulx severely. "Do you not remember that you are the principal cause of this regulation? It is your textbook I particularly want to see, Mr. Derby. Bring it to me at once, Sir."

"But I had rather not, sir," hesitated Derby.

"Perhaps so, sir," replied the Professor; "but you must."

Amid the profound silence and strained expectation of the whole class, Derby slowly walked up to the rostrum, and with elaborate reluctance turned over his textbook. Behold! its pages were innocent of any illustration whatever, and the blank space above the opening chapter bore in capital letters, the legend, "APRIL FOOL." It was the first of April, so the professor although completely shocked by Derby's actions, decided to forgive him for the offense.

After his graduation from the Military Academy, Derby was appointed a brevet second lieutenant in Ordnance and was later transferred to the Topographical Engineers. He served with distinction in the Mexican War and was severely wounded at the battle of Cerro Gordo. For his gallant and meritorious conduct in the encounter he was brevetted a first lieutenant.

While in the Army, Derby regarded writing as an avocation, and in 1853 his art of humor, sketching, and writing made him a success with the American people. During that year, he was the unofficial editor of the *San Diego Herald Newspaper*, and he transformed the sober, Democratic, small-town weekly into a riotous conglomeration of wit, burlesque, and satire devoted to

Captain George H. Derby, Class of 1846.

A typical Derby cartoon, "A Dead Point! — A Dead Set! — A Dead Run!"

the Whig Party. Many of Derby's humorous sketches were published in a volume entitled *Phoenixiana; or Sketches and Burlesque*, which was tremendously popular for a generation. It was after the publication of this book that George Derby assumed the nickname of "John Phoenix." The word "phoenix" may be defined as "a paragon of excellence or beauty." Derby used the name in humorous reference to himself and his writing; it served him well for publicity purposes as a vehicle of self-advertisement.

The Grabhorn Press of San Francisco, California, publishers of the book entitled *Phoenixiana*, has graciously given us permission to reproduce "Squibob's Composition of Armies," which follows. This piece clearly illustrates Derby's unique style of writing.

Mark Twain, a great humorist and lecturer in his own right, was believed to have had the Derby influence in his writings, and there was no question that Derby taught his fellow humorists new tricks of extravagance in expression and thought.

Yes, the Long Gray Line has not only contributed great military leaders, prominent engineers, and distinguished educators to our national development; it has also provided our country with an eminent American humorist!

SQUIBOB'S COMPOSITION OF ARMIES

A new Method of Attack and Defence of Posts

The subject of composition of armies, that of fortification, and the attack and defense of military posts, have for many years been considered of the first importance to the safety and welfare of nations, and have in consequence been elaborately treated of by Vauban, Cormontaigne and other eminent scientific men, of their own and later periods.

With the advance of civilization, refinement and scientific discovery, we should naturally be led to expect new discoveries and improvements in these important branches of the military art.

Such is however by no means the case. Whether a state of peace has operated unfavorably to the prosecution of military research, or that the great minds of modern philosophers are turned exclusively to such sources of discovery as may operate more to their personal emolument than to the benefit of future generations, it is useless to discuss,—true it is, however, that in all essential particulars the art of war remains in precisely the same state that it was left by the savans who wrote upon it half a century ago.

Feeling deeply the necessity of some more perfect means of defence than these comparatively uneducated and uninformed writers have left us, the writer remembering the maxim of the immortal Washington, "In time of peace prepare for war," has devoted himself exclusively for two days to the most close and vigorous research into the principles of the military art, and has finally, by combining the most valuable ideas of the more scientific writers slightly modified by some originality of his own, obtained a system of defence which he thinks more suited to the present advanced stage of science.

This system he would present with becoming deference and humility to the approval of his brother officers, with the hope that they will think it peculiarly adapted to the defence of our own beloved country, when left, in accordance with the message of a late executive, to the tender mercies of armed steamboats and the militia.

And first, with regard to the composition of armies for offensive operations in the field. For this purpose let a body of men between the ages of eighteen and forty-five be selected. These men, after being properly drilled to act in concert, should be armed in the following manner:

1st. Each man to be provided with one of Colt's patent revolving six-barreled rifles, with the necessary ammunition.

2d. A large tin case, perforated with holes on the top, is to be filled with black pepper and suspended by the right side.

3d. A dress cap made of tin and lined with flannel, the top of which is a cylinder containing the material for generating sulphuretted hydrogen gas, with a stop-cock in front, opening by the pressure of a spring, immediately over his right ear. Each man on being enlisted should be furnished with a staunch and well trained bull-dog, which he will take the greatest possible care of, and which he should teach carefully to come and go at his command.

Both men and dogs should be accustomed by frequent drills to the odor of the gas they carry about them, and should be exercised frequently with their pepper pots before being taken into the field. Sneezing on such occasions should be looked upon as a serious military delinquency, and treated accordingly. These preliminary steps being taken, the troops are ready for service.

On the eve of a battle, they will throw up a continuous line in their front, consisting of a parapet and ditch of the usual form and dimensions.

On the advance of the enemy they open a rapid and severe fire with their revolving rifles, which must of course appall and disconcert the enemy. On the slightest symptoms of retreat, the bull-dogs will be loosed and encouraged to charge the retreating foe. This they will do en masse, and seizing the unhappy wretches by the seats of their trowsers, will delay their progress or drag them back within close rifle shot. This will generally decide the affair. If, however, in consequence of vast numbers or determined bravery, the enemy advance to the trench, a warm fire must be kept up.

On coming to close quarters, the men will use their pepper pots vigorously. Nothing can withstand this system,—with eyes smarting and blinded with pepper, noses offended with the stench of the parapet, deafened by the barking of the dogs and incessantly annoyed by their sharp and tenacious gripe, the enemy, though composed of the best materials that ever made up an army, must give way and fall an easy prey, in their torturing retreat, to our victorious arms.

When flying artillery is used in connection with these troops, it will consist of four and six pound fieldpieces, carefully strapped on the backs of stout jackasses and pointed to the rear. These being fired the recoil will arouse all the natural obstinacy of the animal, who, thinking he is pushed forward, will instantly move stern first, with incredible celerity, towards the enemy. When a retreat is ordered, the men serving the gun will pull the beast's tail, who will immediately change his motion and rush forward with impetuosity. It is thus that man shows his supremacy over the brute creation, in rendering even their evil dispositions subservient to his designs.

"Le Cadet," drawn by Cadet George H. Derby, 1842.

PROMINENT "GOATS"
OF
THE U.S. MILITARY ACADEMY

The origin of the frequently used word "goat" at the Military Academy is difficult to determine. It has always been known that it meant simply a cadet or cadets academically near the bottom of the class. Prior to "goat," the word "Immortal" always signified the lowest ranking man or men in the class.

A search of the archival holdings revealed that the earliest use of the word was in a "Hundredth Night" pamphlet issued by the United States Corps of Cadets in February, 1886. It reads as follows:

"What feature of the Instructor of the Immortals in Spanish resembles his Section?

"Answer — His Beard; it is (a) goatee, and so is his Section!"

It is the intention here to recognize a certain select group of graduates who ranked last in their respective classes and yet attained recognition for some significant contribution to American life.

George A. Custer is without a doubt the most controversial and widely known of all the "goats" in the history of the Military Academy. From the time of the Battle of Little Big Horn military strategists, historians, and people from all walks of life have expressed their views of the tragic event and the characters involved in the battle. Some are of the opinion that Marcus Reno was the "scapegoat" who was used to cover up General Custer's famous blunder. Other scholarly researchers feel

Cadet George A. Custer, Class of June, 1861.

Custer's superiors were at fault because the estimates of actual Indian strength were completely in error. Where 10,000 Indians were supposedly on a reservation, only 4,000 could be accounted for. The balance had joined other renegade Indians from other reservations to mass such a force that Custer and his command were completely overwhelmed. In any event, probably more has been written about George A. Custer and the Battle of Little Big Horn than any other incident in American history.

General George E. Pickett, ranked at the foot of the Class of 1846, a class in which Thomas J. (Stonewall) Jackson was in all probability the most distinguished member.

On July 3, 1863, at Gettysburg, General Pickett advanced his command over half a mile of broken ground against withering artillery and musket fire. With the precision of parade drill they descended one slope, ascended the next, and, with unmatched courage and individual gallantry, assaulted the formidable Union line, only to be forced back in defeat. Although Pickett lost nearly 75 percent of his men in the engagement, and was soundly defeated, he was immortalized by this battle, known familiarly as "Pickett's Charge."

General John J. Abert, Class of 1811, was appointed chief of the Topographical Bureau, which was created as an independent branch of the War Department in June 1831. As chief of the Bureau, he was largely responsible for initiating and guiding the topographic surveys of the United States, particularly in the West. He had the task of planning, organizing, and integrating the voluminous textual and cartographic products of these surveys. Abert's awareness of the essential details of the geographic landscape and his requirements for its adequate description place him in the forefront of the American geographers of his time. His energy, his boundless capacity for work, and his abilities at organization were largely responsible for making the Topographical Bureau perhaps the most valuable respository of topographic description of the United States for this period.

General Rene E. DeRussy, Class of 1812, has the distinction of being the only West Pointer to graduate at the foot of his class and yet attain the prestigious position of the Superintendent, U.S. Military Academy. DeRussy entered the Academy in March 1807 and remained in the Corps of Engineers until his death on November 23, 1865. He served as superintendent from 1833 through 1838, relieving Colonel Sylvanus Thayer.

One of the most unique graduates to hold the last slot was George P. Ahern, Class of 1882. Ahern personally felt after graduation that the routine of Army life had small appeal to his free and enterprising spirit. His desire was to see new country, to do new things, and to be of use to his fellow men. During the Spanish-American War, Captain Ahern had won the Silver Star and was cited for gallantry in action. He later received a serious leg injury which prevented him from active service in the Philippine Insurrection. As a result, he later organized the Insular Bureau of Forestry in the Philippines and served under Mr. Gifford Pinchot, former director of the Forest Service in the United States. In commenting on Captain Ahern's life, Mr. Pinchot remarked that Ahern's remarkable contribution to forestry in the East and in the West was all the more notable for the reason that he was self-trained in this field. Because of his distinguished services to the cause of forestry management in America, he was one of the few men elected to become a fellow of the Society of American Foresters. It is not often that a military man is able to accomplish such an outstanding record of public service in a civilian field such as forestry.

Lieutenant Powhatan H. Clarke ranked number 37 in a class of 37 members which graduated on June 15, 1884. Clarke was a recipient of the Congressional Medal of Honor for his action at Penito Mountains, Mexico against the hostile Apache Indians in May 1886. During the engagement an enlisted soldier was severely wounded and lay disabled under a sharp fire from the Indians. Lieutenant Clarke distinguished himself by rushing forward; at the risk of his life, he carried the disabled soldier to a place of safety. After the incident, Clarke remarked, "I was scared to death but the man called to me, and you know, I couldn't leave him to be shot to death."

Charles Young, Class of 1889, was the third black man to graduate from the U.S. Military Academy. It is understandable that in 1885 Young had many obstacles to overcome as a cadet; however, after great perseverance his classmates began to acknowledge and respect his fine traits of character. Just prior

Major General G.E. Pickett, Class of 1846.

Colonel John J. Abert, Class of 1811.

Colonel Rene E. DeRussy, Class of 1812.

Cadet George P. Ahern, Class of 1882.

Cadet Powhatan H. Clarke, Class of 1884.

Cadet Charles Young, Class of 1889.

to the graduation of his class in 1889, Cadet Young was declared deficient in Engineering by the Academic Board and was nearly dismissed. Through the efforts of certain instructors who recognized his steadfast perseverance, he was permitted to remain and be tutored by the very instructor who had declared him deficient. The instructor was none other than General George W. Goethals who later achieved fame for his efforts in the construction of the Panama Canal.

In the United States Army, as at West Point, Charles Young demonstrated qualities of mind and temperament which were unquestionably remarkable.

It should be noted here that the long standing tradition of the General Order of Merit system which originated at the Academy in 1818 was abolished with the graduation of the Class of 1978. The procedure was originally based on the academic standings of cadets, to which were added components for leadership and conduct. With the current change only the top five percent of the class receive their diplomas by order of academic standing; the remainder of the graduating class receive their diplomas in alphabetical order. Thus the custom of designating a specific cadet as "the goat" of his particular class is no longer possible at the U.S. Military Academy.

Major General William C. Westmoreland congratulates Cadet Clyde P. Gibson, the last man in the Class of 1972.

A SELECT GROUP OF
HONOR GRADUATES FROM
THE U.S. MILITARY ACADEMY
1802-1950

The author would be remiss if he did not in turn honor a limited number of "academic hives" (Number one graduates) who attained world notoriety in varied fields of endeavor. A survey of the top ranking graduates through the years shows that a total of five held the distinction of serving as superintendent of their Alma Mater. A further analysis reveals that the major portion of past honor graduates have also been recipients of the Congressional Medal of Honor; and they have been daring Indian fighters; renowned engineers, and gallant military leaders.

One of the most frequently asked questions the UMSA Archives receives from school students is "Who graduated Number One in the Class of 1829, ahead of General Robert E. Lee, the number two ranked cadet?"

It is the author's opinion that the following number one graduates merit particular acknowledgement because of their dedication to the Military Academy, and more importantly, to our country.

Joseph G. Swift
Class of 1802

Joseph Gardner Swift had the unique honor of being the first graduate of the Military Academy. Actually, it would be stretching the point to say that Swift was the top ranking graduate in his class because no class rank was established until the

General Joseph G. Swift, Class of 1802, and the first graduate of the U.S. Military Academy.

administration of Sylvanus Thayer as superintendent. Prior to 1818 the graduates were arranged in order of dates of first commission. Swift was appointed a cadet of artillerists and engineers in the Army by President John Adams on May 12, 1800. During the summer of 1801, the Secretary of War informed the little army at West Point that President Thomas Jefferson had directed the establishment of a military school for the education of cadets. Swift reported for duty on October 14, 1801 and graduated October 12, 1802 with Simon M. Levy, the only other cadet to graduate in the class.

Although Swift was commissioned an officer at the Military Academy before the class rank policy originated, it is considered appropriate to cite his name merely on the basis of being the first graduate of the Military Academy.

Richard Delafield
Class of 1818

Richard Delafield was the first cadet to whom a standing according to merit was assigned. From 1818 until the recent change in 1978, class rank has been one of the distinguishing features of the Academy. It has proven to be an excellent method to instill in the minds of new cadets the idea that determination and perseverance are required to attain the top goal of excellence.

Delafield served in the U.S. Army for forty-eight years and in that time he exhibited conspicious executive abilities. He held the position as superintendent of his alma mater for two tenures of office, totaling over eleven years. In each of his tours of duty as superintendent he instituted many major improvements for the betterment of the West Point community.

As superintendent it has been stated that "Delafield embellished the Point with roads and structures of various uses, and he had the credit of doing more with a dollar than any other man in the Army."

Dennis H. Mahan
Class of 1824

Dennis H. Mahan was probably the most eminent professor in the entire history of the U.S. Military Academy.

As the professor of engineering, he was responsible for insuring that the cadets were properly instructed in the history of military warfare. He received his early training in the science of military engineering at the Military Academy under the watchful eye of Superintendent Sylvanus Thayer. After graduating first in his class, Mahan was sent to Europe for advanced military engineering schooling at Metz, France. He returned to the U.S. Military Academy with a vast knowledge of strategy in warfare and instilled this information in cadets for generations to come.

Professor Mahan served at the Military Academy for forty-one years and his service not only made an impact on the teaching methods at the Academy, but on the entire Army as well.

His loyalty to his country, its Army, and particularly to the U.S. Military Academy was extremely strong. In many instances he defended the Academy against those who constantly criticized the administration for various insignificant happenings.

Isaac I. Stevens
Class of 1839

Isaac I. Stevens was a native of Andover, Massachusetts. Prior to his admission to the Military Academy, he had excelled in academics in his local high school. He attended Phillips's Academy and after a year received his appointment to West Point.

His services in the Mexican War were highly creditable, and he served as the engineer adjutant on General Winfield Scott's staff. He displayed a combination of sound judgment and "cool daring" in the battles of Contreras, Churubusco, and Chapultepec, for which he was brevetted the ranks of captain and major.

In 1849, Stevens was appointed as an executive assistant in the United States Coast Survey. However, he decided to resign from the Army in 1853 to accept the governorship of the new Washington Territory. It was through the efforts and knowledge

Professor Dennis H. Mahan, Class of 1824.

Brigadier General Isaac I. Stevens, Class of 1839.

of General Stevens and other prominent men that the opening of the West became a reality.

Paul Hebert
Class of 1840

As a youth, Paul Hebert was an apt scholar, displaying a ready capacity for the acquisition of knowledge, especially in the exact sciences of mathematics and physics. It was this talent coupled with perseverance and untiring application that enabled him to win top honors in his class.

Professor Charles Davies was the professor of mathematics during the time of Paul and Louis Hebert's cadetship, and he made the following statement concerning the Hebert cousins. "It has been ever to me a curious thing that the French mind always is so apt in Mathematics. The general tendency of the French nature is popularly supposed to be frivolous. But all our best mathematics come from France. The Hebert boys bear out the theory that the French genius is essentially mathematical."

Paul Hebert later became the governor of the State of Louisiana when only 35 years of age.

James B. McPherson
Class of 1853

As a boy James B. McPherson was a special favorite with young and old alike. He grew into a bright and manly individual and always maintained the top position in his class academically.

McPherson was admitted to the Military Academy in 1849 and graduated in 1853, standing number one in a class of fifty-two members. He then spent approximately seven years constructing fortifications in New York, Boston, and California.

At the outbreak of the Civil War, Colonel McPherson was assigned to General Grant's staff as chief of engineers. He was considered by Grant to be one of the most able commanders of the Federal troops during the war. After serving brilliantly at the battles of Corinth and Vicksburg he was made a brigadier general in the Regular Army and commander of the District of

Major General James B. McPherson, Class of 1853.

Brigadier General Paul O. Hebert, Class of 1840.

Vicksburg. Unfortunately, General McPherson was later killed in action at the Battle of Atlanta on July 22, 1864.

General U.S. Grant in writing a letter of condolence to General McPherson's grandmother expressed his feelings of sympathy in the following manner:

Headquarters Armies of the
United States, City Point, Virginia

August 10, 1864

My dear Madam:

Your very welcome letter of the 3rd instant has reached me. I am glad to know the relatives of the lamented Major General McPherson are aware of the more than friendship existing between him and myself. A nation grieves at the loss of one so dear to our nation's cause. It is a selfish grief, because the nation had more to expect from him than from anyone living. I join in this selfish grief, and add the grief of personal love for the departed. He formed for some time one of my military family. I knew him well. To know him was but to love him. It may be some consolation to you, his aged grandmother, to know that every officer and every soldier who served under your grandson felt the highest reverence for his patriotism, his zeal, his great, almost unequalled ability, his amiability, and all the many virtues that can adorn a commander. Your bereavement is great, but cannot exceed mine.

Yours truly,

U.S. Grant
Lieutenant General

Henry A. DuPont
Class of May 1861

Henry A. DuPont, the top ranking graduate in the Class of May 1861, had a distinguished military career. During the Civil War he participated in many major battles. For his conspicuous service at Cedar Creek, Virginia on October 19, 1864, he received the Congressional Medal of Honor. The citation reads in part: "By his distinguished gallantry, and voluntary exposure to the enemy's fire at a critical moment, when the Union line had been broken, encouraged his men to stand to their guns, checked the advance of the enemy, and brought off most of his pieces."

Cadet Henry A. DuPont, Class of 1861.

Colonel DuPont was an ardent advocate of military training and felt his life was greatly influenced by it. He once stated that "as a young man I received a military training, as did my father before me, and, so far as I am concerned, have always considered that my entrance to the United States Military Academy was the turning point of my life, recognizing as I do that what little I have been able to accomplish in my time has been very largely influenced by the military regime of my early days."

Ranald S. Mackenzie
Class of 1862

Ranald S. Mackenzie is probably one of the most underrated graduates from the U.S. Military Academy. As a youth he was very shy and reserved, his speech was slow and a little indistinct, his manner diffident and hesitating. When he received word of his appointment to the Academy, nearly all of his acquaintances and relations expected him to fail at West Point. However, his instructors at the Military Academy held an entirely different opinion, and they alone understood the boy's quiet courage and uncommon ability. To them no honor that came to Ranald S. Mackenzie could ever be a surprise. His sterling qualities of heart and mind soon made him a great favorite in his class and very popular with the entire Corps of Cadets.

Upon graduating in 1862, he was almost immediately thrust into battle at Manassas, and he subsequently fought at Chancellorsville, Gettysburg, and at Cold Harbor where he took command of his regiment at the early age of twenty-three. His advancement during the Civil War was phenomenal, he held higher rank during the war than any man in his class, and higher rank than any other officer whose military life began in the second year of the war. When Mackenzie was promoted to the rank of colonel of the Forty-first Infantry, he was only twenty-six years old and, except for General Galusha Pennypacker, the youngest colonel in the U.S. Army.

At the conclusion of the Civil War, Mackenzie was assigned to service with the 4th Cavalry in the southwest where he took the leading part in the campaigns against the marauding Indians. It was from his actions in these campaigns that MacKenzie received notoriety and fame. The Indians referred to him as

Cadet Ranald S. Mackenzie, Class of 1862.

"Bad Hand" because of the loss of several fingers, the result of an injury received during the Civil War.

Ranald S. Mackenzie's lack of worldwide fame can be attributed to his tempermental aversion to publicity. All of the major military operations under his command were followed by brief reports. Instead of blowing his own horn he devoted all his energies to the profession of a soldier.

Ranald S. Mackenzie was truly a remarkable man!

Douglas MacArthur
Class of 1903

A friend of General MacArthur's once stated that MacArthur was a marked man insofar as his academic abilities were concerned at the Military Academy. Looking back to those times, it becomes clear that many of the characteristics which made him the great American that he was, must have come to fruition during his cadet days. It was then, as in later years, that he rose to the responsibilities of the position or office he was filling.

General MacArthur returned as superintendent of the Military Academy in 1919 when conditions were generally in a turmoil. During World War I the early graduation of classes had seriously jeopardized the Academy. A large majority of the nation's population felt that we had won the war to end all wars. This in turn made some congressmen ask the question: "Why do we need a military academy?" The pacifists were naturally answering: "Abolish West Point!" General MacArthur adequately answered these ridiculous critics by implementing vast and constructive changes. MacArthur's vision of an evolutionary change included the return of distinguished young officers for assignment either to the tactical or the academic departments.

A classmate of General MacArthur's so aptly stated that "If Sylvanus Thayer was the Father of the Military Academy, then Douglas MacArthur was its Savior."

Brigadier General Douglas MacArthur, Class of 1903.

THE LEGENDARY BENNY HAVENS

Benny Havens was a familiar figure at West Point for more than fifty years. He established a tavern at Buttermilk Falls, (presently the Village of Highland Falls), where he accommodated the mischievous cadets by selling them contraband, particularly alcoholic beverages. In all probability the two cadets who most frequently visited the premises were Edgar Allan Poe and Jefferson Davis. Poe is reported to have casually remarked that Benny Havens "was the only congenial soul in the entire God-forsaken place."

The cadets admiration for Havens led to the title of the familiar tune entitled "Benny Havens, Oh!" The first stanza reads as follows:

> Come, fill your glasses, fellows, and stand up in a row
> To singing sentimentally, we're going for to go;
> In the Army there's sobriety, promotion's very slow,
> So we'll sing our reminiscences of Benny Havens, Oh!
> Oh, Benny Havens, oh! Oh! Benny Havens, oh!
> So we'll sing our reminiscences of Benny Havens, oh!

While recently examining an early record series in the USMA Archives the author uncovered an interesting report entitled "Statement of Facts Concerning Mr. Benjamin Havens," written by the then Police Sergeant Silvester (Bum) Owens. Since Havens has been regarded as a part of the famous legends and traditions at West Point, it is felt the report is worth including in a collection of West Point lore. The report of Sergeant Owens to Superintendent Henry Brewerton follows:

STATEMENT OF FACTS
CONCERNING MR. BENJAMIN HAVENS

by

Police Sergeant Silvester (Bum) Owens
November 11, 1847

I, the undersigned, Sergeant S. Owens, on the afternoon of the 8th instant, near the time of the landing of the Albany boat, was going down the dock hill on my way to the dock, when I perceived John Van Voorhies, the West Point ferryman, beckoning to me; on my arrival at the ferry dock, I perceived Benjamin Havens in his long boat, apparently designing to land some two or three females he had in said boat, at the ferrymans landing. The said Havens seeing me, slowly pulled out and passed up the river. I asked the Corporal of the guard "if he knew Havens' long boat," he answered "I do." I then asked him "if he knew whether Havens intended landing," he replied that he thought he intended landing below the floating dock," and that he walked toward him & he bore off." He also told me that when said Havens passed the dock, Mr. Kinsley asked him "where he was going?" He, the said Havens replied "that he was going to Newburgh & asked Mr. Kinsley if he wished to go along? The reason of my asking the said Corporal these questions was because I wished to learn whether the said Havens was going to Cold Spring as I thought it would be better for me not to go there, if he had, and I mentioned this to the Corporal.

The Corporal then told me that Mr. Kinsley said, "that Havens did not intend landing, and that he, the said Havens only wished to bother them." But Sergeant L'ameraux has since told me, that he, the said L'ameraux was on the dock at the time Havens passed, and that he the said Havens was not spoken to by any person on the dock. I then started for Cold Spring in company with Sergeant Twiss. We landed at the Cold Spring dock, and I proceeded to the store of Iacox & Co. While in said store, the said Havens entered, approached me, and told me "to come to the door since he wanted to talk to me." I went to the door with him, where he was very profane and abusive. He then told me to go with him, pointing to the road leading to the foundry. I replied that "I did not wish to have anything to do with him." I then went back into the store; the said Havens followed me in, calling me "a damned son of a bitch," "a damn lousy soldier," and at the same time spitting into my face. He then took hold of my coat, and with his finger nails, scratched my face, then caught me by the nose, and ears, pulling me around. I, during this time, offered no violence toward him or no insulting language whatever, but endeavored to escape from him, and begged him to leave me alone.

I then told him that the reason he abused me was "because I did nothing but my duty and that he had been in the habit of smuggling liquor

Benny Havens, a legendary figure who sold contraband to Edgar A. Poe, Jefferson Davis, and a host of other distinguished West Pointers.

on the shores of West Point and that his trade was now ended." I then slapped my hands on the side of my pantaloons and said "Mr. Havens, I will not say Mr., but Havens, as long as these stripes are on my legs and as long as it is my duty to protect those shores from smugglers, I am bound to do it." To which, Havens answered, "I have got fellows looking out for you, and I have a gun ready for you, and I will fetch you with it." I then turned around to the bystanders, and apologized to the proprietor of the store and told them the reason why Havens was so abusive. The Proprietor then told Havens "to go out-doors." He, the said Havens then departed, and a few minutes after, I in company with Sergeant Twiss returned home.

The following persons were present during the last above transaction, viz: Iacox, William Wright, Daniel Caldwell, Mr. Mason, Judge Warren, and some other persons, whose names are unknown to me.

I also this afternoon, went over to Cold Spring again and while in the Tin Shop of Mr. Pelton, waiting for him to finish some work for me, I saw the aforesaid Havens pass, having in his hand a club apparently 3 feet in length. In a few moments, the said Havens, came into Pelton's store, and stepped towards me, I looked him in the face and said, "Mr. Havens", to which he made no reply. When I got ready to leave, Mr. Pelton stepped into his finishing shop, leaving Havens and myself in the store. I then went to the door, Mr. Havens standing nearby and looking at me very sharply, I then said, "Mr. Havens, you don't want anything of me, do you?" I being fearful of him, left the store quickly and hastily started down the street, when the said Havens persued me, with his club raised. I then saw that he had the advantage of me, as he was above me, and I stopped to fend off the blow. He, then with his club struck me twice & I, with my arm attempted to fend off the blows, when he, with the club, using both hands, with a full blow struck me on the side. I then caught him by the arms and held him until persons came to the rescue, when they told me "to let him go." I did so, I then, to prevent him striking me again, picked up his club which was lying on the ground. He then told me to give him the club, as it was his. I then told him I would not, as he would only strike me with it again." Mr. McCabe interfered and told me to give Havens the club, and that he, the said Havens should not again strike me. Some one of them took the club from me and gave it to Havens, when he, the said Havens, passing around through the crowd, I watching the club. He unexpectedly to me, struck me with his fist on the side of my head, all this time using very profane and abusive language. He then being told by the bystanders not to interfere with any more, went away. I then returned home and as I started I perceived Havens in a boat laying off near the dock.

The following persons were present during the last above afrray, viz: Iacox, a tailor who saw him strike me with the club and Devenport, a harness maker saw him strike me with his fist, and many others whose names I do not know, but can ascertain who they were.

The author has also found the following document relating to Benny Havens's activities in an earlier period:

Military Academy   Engineer Department
Orders No. 19   Washington, August 29, 1825

At the same court was tried Cadet Jefferson Davis on the following charges & specifications, Viz

Charge 1st — Violating the 1415 paragraph of the General Army Regulations.

Specification — In this that the said Cadet Davis did on Sunday, 31st July 1825, go beyond the limits prescribed to Cadets at West Point without permission.

Charge 2d — Violating the 1408 paragraph of the General Army Regulations.

Specification 1st — In this, that the said Cadet Davis did on Sunday, 31st July 1825, at some place in the vicinity of West Point, drink spirituous & intoxicating liquor.

Specification 2d — In this, that the said Cadet Davis on Sunday, 31st July 1825, did go to a public house or place where spirituous liquors are sold: kept by one Benjamin Havens at or near Buttermilk Falls & distant about two miles from the Post of West Point.

The prisoner pleaded to the 1st charge & its specification guilty, to the 1st specification 2d charge not guilty, to the 2d specification 2d charge guilty, to the 2d charge guilty of violating so much of the 1408th paragraph of the General Army Regulations as prohibits going to a public house or place where liquors are sold & not guilty of the remainder.

The Court after mature deliberation on the testimony adduced find the prisoner Cadet Jefferson Davis guilty of both the 1st & 2d charges preferred against him and their specifications.

The Court sentences him to be dismissed from the service of the United States, but in consideration of his former good conduct respectfully recommend the remission of said sentence.

/s/
Alex. Macomb
Maj. Gen. & Inspector
of the Military Academy

Post Order Book No. 3, (1823-1825)

CHRISTY MATHEWSON
AND
THE CORPS OF CADETS

Last Spring my youngest son, Danny, aged seven, tactfully conned me into having a game of "catch" in our backyard. I use the word "conned" because he has that unique way, as most young boys do, of twisting their fathers' arm to obtain their specific wishes. After consenting, and then chasing the ball a number of times around our neighbor's picket fence, I cleverly explained to him that I thought he was becoming exhausted! He quickly responded with the comment, "Gee Dad, you haven't the pep that Mom has!" I hurriedly walked into the kitchen, picked two soft drinks from the refrigerator, and sat down with him to discuss baseball. It is truly amazing how much knowledge a young boy can have on certain subjects; in Danny's case, it was baseball. In the course of our conversation he recited the complete New York Yankee roster, and informed me that "Catfish" Hunter was having a bad year. He then asked who was considered to be the greatest pitcher of all time? It was rather difficult for me to give him an accurate answer. I recalled as a youth hearing of, or reading about, the famous exploits of pitchers named Walter Johnson, "Christy" Mathewson, and "Lefty" Grove. It also brought back memories of my personally seeing such pitching stars as "Red" Ruffing, "Spud" Chandler, and Whitlow Wyatt. I finally ended our discussion by remarking that Bob Feller of the Cleveland Indians was probably the greatest pitcher of all time. My answer seemed to satisfy his interest and our parley ended on a happy note.

Approximately a month after our baseball chat, I received a letter at the USMA Archives from an "old-time baseball buff" who desired a verification that "Christy" Mathewson of New

"Christy" Mathewson of the New York Giants. John J. McGraw regarded Mathewson as the player who had everything.

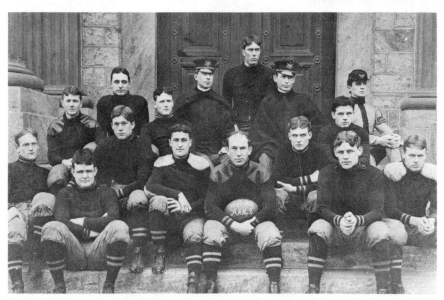

Army Football Team, 1902. Cadet Douglas MacArthur, Manager of the Team, is in cadet uniform, back row, far right.

York Giant fame had at one time instructed the Army Baseball Team's pitching staff. It should be noted that to baseball enthusiasts the name Mathewson is as meaningful as the name of Henry Ford to the auto industry. After combing a number of archival sources I was elated to turn up the information requested. The record revealed that Mathewson did, indeed, tutor the Army pitchers. On January 15, 1908, Lieutenant Joseph Barnes, then serving as the secretary of the Army Athletic Association, reported that one of the expenditures authorized by the council for the baseball season of 1908 was the payment of $75.00 per week and expenses (board and quarters) to Mathewson for his services as the coach for the pitching squad. His three-week stint as an instructor to the youthful cadets was performed in the cadet gymnasium and terminated in February, just prior to his departure for spring training with the beloved Giants. It was unfortunate that Mathewson did not have the opportunity to work with the new plebes who entered the Corps in March 1908, because they possessed far greater potential than any of the upperclassmen on the squad at the time.

The excellent choice of the Athletic Council in obtaining the services of Mathewson was in all probability based on two major factors. First, the council knew that Mathewson's masterful pitching performance in the 1905 World Series when he hurled three shutout victories for the Giants over the Philadelphia Athletics was recognized throughout America. Secondly, and evidently the most significant factor, was that Mathewson had been a college man, that he had exhibited traits of the perfect gentleman, and that he possessed superb natural athletic talent. It was because of these remarkable attributes that educators could point to him as the perfect model for other college athletes to emulate. Hence, the members of the Athletic Council were quick to realize the importance of hiring Mathewson as a pitching coach. They knew that his presence at West Point would be an inspiring influence to the entire Corps of Cadets.

A short time later I discovered that Mathewson's earliest association with the cadets had begun on November 17, 1900. He had obtained a scholarship from Bucknell College at Lewisburg, Pennsylvania for his varied athletic achievement. Interestingly enough, the scheduled opponent for the Army Football Team of 1900 on November 17th was Bucknell. A summary of

John J. McGraw, Manager of the New York Giants, 1902-1932.

the memorable game as described in the *New York Times* revealed that Bucknell had the ball on Army's thirty-five yard line in the first half when their coach decided to have Mathewson attempt a field goal. He quickly met the challenge by splitting the goal post, and that enabled Bucknell to lead at the end of the half. Bucknell's hope of an upset was short-lived, since Army, with All-American Paul Bunker, dominated the play in the second half and won the game by 18-10.

An example of "Christy" Mathewson's impact on the cadets can best be documented through the reminiscences of General Douglas MacArthur. He related a conversation he once held with the hard-nosed disciplinarian, John J. McGraw, former Manager of the Giants. He asked McGraw whom he considered to be the best fielding pitcher he had ever known. MacArthur remarked that he already knew McGraw regarded Mathewson as the greatest throwing pitcher of all-time, and he was not surprised when the "Little Napoleon of Baseball" replied "Mathewson" to his question. The General then concluded his remarks by stating that as a cadet he had seen Mathewson play the greatest single game at fullback that he ever witnessed on the Plain at West Point.

As a result of my findings I was later able to tell my son affirmatively, that "Christy" Mathewson was undoubtedly the greatest pitcher of all time!

THE YOUNG LIEUTENANTS

Approximately fifteen years ago I had the good fortune to make the acquaintance of an exceptional officer of the U.S. Army. His excellent leadership qualities and outstanding military career had long been acknowledged throughout the military and civilian circles. The purpose of his visit to West Point was to examine any materials relating to the cadet careers of George A. Custer and Marcus A. Reno, both being leading characters in the controversial disaster at the Battle of the Little Big Horn. The study of the strategic battle had always been one of the chief interests of the visiting officer, and after his retirement from the Army he had the necessary time to research the subject more thoroughly.

As a result of his short visit we later began to correspond, and in almost every letter I received he always managed to insert some humorous incident or event relating to his own lengthy Army career. Rereading these old letters recently, turned up an amusing anecdote which I feel should be included in a collection of West Point lore. My only excuse for telling the supposed incident is that, having once been in the prime of life at twenty-one, I can sympathize with the lieutenants' complete dismay.

The event took place in the early 1900s with the arrival of two young lieutenants assigned to The Presidio of San Francisco. After a few days of arduous duty, they decided to have a night on the town on the famous Barbary Coast. At sun-up the following morning they were standing at the corner of Pacific and Van Ness waiting for the streetcar, when a voluptuous young lady approached and stopped beside them; she too was waiting for transportation. One of the lieutenants began to eye her. Finally he walked out in front, made a very low bow, and asked: "Madam, can you tell me where I can get the car for the

Presidio?" The young lady replied: "You'll get it right in the ass, if you don't get out of the street!" I leave the resulting confusion to your imagination.

SUPERINTENDENTS OF THE UNITED STATES MILITARY ACADEMY

No.	Name	Class	Rank When Appointed	Term of Service From	To
1	Jonathan Williams	—	Major Corps of Engineers	Apr. 15, 1802	June 20, 1803
2	Jonathan Williams[1]	—	Lt Col Corps of Engineers	Apr. 19, 1805	July 31, 1812
3	Joseph G. Swift	1802	Col Corps of Engineers	July 31, 1812	Mar. 24, 1814
4	Alden Partridge	1806	Capt Corps of Engineers	Mar. 24, 1814	July 28, 1817
5	Sylvanus Thayer	1808	Capt Corps of Engineers	July 28, 1817	July 1, 1833
6	Rene E. DeRussy	1812	Major Corps of Engineers	July 1, 1833	Sept. 1, 1838
7	Richard Delafield	1818	Major Corps of Engineers	Sept. 1, 1838	Aug. 15, 1845
8	Henry Brewerton	1819	Capt Corps of Engineers	Aug. 15, 1845	Sept. 1, 1852
9	Robert E. Lee	1829	Capt Corps of Engineers	Sept. 1, 1852	Mar. 31, 1855
10	John G. Barnard	1833	Capt Corps of Engineers	Mar. 31, 1855	Sept. 8, 1856
11	Richard Delafield	1818	Major Corps of Engineers	Sept. 8, 1856	Jan. 23, 1861
12	Pierre G.T. Beauregard	1838	Capt Corps of Engineers	Jan. 23, 1861	Jan. 28, 1861
13	Richard Delafield	1818	Major Corps of Engineers	Jan. 28, 1861	Mar. 1, 1861
14	Alexander H. Bowman	1825	Major Corps of Engineers	Mar. 1, 1861	July 8, 1864
15	Zealous B. Tower	1841	Major Corps of Engineers	July 8, 1864	Sept. 8, 1864
16	George W. Cullum	1833	Lt Col Corps of Engineers	Sept. 8, 1864	Aug. 28, 1866
17	Thomas G. Pitcher	1845	Colonel 44th Infantry	Aug. 28, 1866	Sept. 1, 1871
18	Thomas H. Ruger	1854	Colonel 18th Infantry	Sept. 1, 1871	Sept. 1, 1876
19	John M. Schofield	1853	Major General	Sept. 1, 1876	Jan. 21, 1881
20	Oliver O. Howard	1854	Brigadier General	Jan. 21, 1881	Sept. 1, 1882
21	Wesley Merritt	1860	Colonel 5th Cavalry	Sept. 1, 1882	July 1, 1887
22	John G. Parke	1849	Col Corps of Engineers	Aug. 28, 1887	June 24, 1889
23	John M. Wilson	1860	Lt Col Corps of Engineers	Aug. 26, 1889	Mar. 31, 1893
24	Oswald H. Ernst	1864	Major Corps of Engineers	Mar. 31, 1893	Aug. 21, 1898
25	Albert L. Mills	1879	1st Lt 1st Cavalry	Aug. 22, 1898	Aug. 31, 1906

No.	Name	Year	Rank		
26	Hugh L. Scott	1876	Major 14th Cavalry	Aug. 31, 1906	Aug. 31, 1910
27	Thomas H. Barry	1877	Major General	Aug. 31, 1910	Aug. 31, 1912
28	Clarence P. Townsley	1881	Col Coast Artillery Corps	Aug. 31, 1912	June 30, 1916
29	John Biddle	1881	Col Corps of Engineers	July 1, 1916	May 31, 1917
30	Samuel E. Tillman	1869	Colonel US Army	June 13, 1917	June 11, 1919
31	Douglas MacArthur	1903	Brigadier General	June 12, 1919	June 30, 1922
32	Fred W. Sladen	1890	Brigadier General	July 1, 1922	Mar. 23, 1926
33	Merch B. Stewart	1896	Brigadier General	Mar. 24, 1926	Oct. 5, 1927
34	Edwin B. Winans	1891	Major General	Oct. 23, 1927	Feb. 25, 1928
35	William R. Smith	1892	Major General	Feb. 26, 1928	Apr. 30, 1932
36	William D. Connor	1897	Major General	May 1, 1932	Jan. 17, 1938
37	Jay L. Benedict	1904	Brigadier General	Feb. 5, 1938	Nov. 17, 1940
38	Robert L. Eichelberger	1909	Brigadier General	Nov. 18, 1940	Jan. 12, 1942
39	Francis B. Wilby	1905	Major General	Jan. 13, 1942	Sept. 4, 1945
40	Maxwell D. Taylor	1922	Major General	Sept. 4, 1945	Jan. 28, 1949
41	Bryant E. Moore	1917	Major General	Jan. 28, 1949	Jan. 17, 1951
42	Frederick A. Irving	1917	Major General	Feb. 1, 1951	Aug. 31, 1954
43	Blackshear M. Bryan	1922	Lieutenant General	Sept. 3, 1954	July 15, 1956
44	Garrison H. Davidson	1927	Major General	July 15, 1956	July 1, 1960
45	Wm. C. Westmoreland	1936	Major General	July 1, 1960	June 25, 1963
46	James B. Lampert	1936	Major General	June 28, 1963	Jan. 6, 1966
47	Donald V. Bennett	1940	Major General	Jan. 10, 1966	June 15, 1968
48	Samuel W. Koster	1942	Major General	June 26, 1968	Mar. 22, 1970
49	William A. Knowlton	1943	Major General	Mar. 23, 1970	July 18, 1974
50	Sidney B. Berry	1948	Major General	July 19, 1974	June 13, 1977
51	Andrew J. Goodpaster	1939	Lieutenant General	June 13, 1977	

[1]Williams resigned June 20, 1803, on a point of command. Pending its settlement, no permanent Superintendent of the Military Academy was appointed until April 19, 1805, when he again returned to service as Chief Engineer. During the interim the command devolved upon the senior officer of the Corps of Engineers present for duty.

COMMANDANTS OF CADETS OF THE UNITED STATES MILITARY ACADEMY

No.	Name	Class	Rank When Appointed	Term of Service From	To
1	George W. Gardiner	1814	2nd Lieut Corps of Arty	15 Sep 1817	2 Apr 1818
2	John Bliss	–	Captain 6th Infantry	2 Apr 1818	15 Jan 1819
3	John R. Bell	1812	Captain Light Artillery	8 Feb 1819	17 Mar 1820
4	William J. Worth	–	Captain 2nd Infantry	17 Mar 1820	2 Dec 1828
5	Ethan A. Hitchcock	1817	Captain 1st Infantry	13 Mar 1829	24 Jun 1833
6	John Fowle	–	Major 3rd Infantry	10 Jul 1833	31 Mar 1838
7	Charles F. Smith	1825	1st Lieut 2nd Artillery	1 Apr 1838	7 Sep 1842
8	John A. Thomas	1833	1st Lieut 3rd Artillery	1 Sep 1842	14 Dec 1845
9	Bradford R. Alden	1831	Captain 4th Infantry	14 Dec 1845	7 Nov 1852
10	Robert S. Garnett	1841	Captain 6th Infantry	1 Nov 1852	31 Jul 1854
11	William H.T. Walker	1837	Captain 6th Infantry	31 Jul 1854	27 May 1856
12	William J. Hardee	1838	Major 2nd Cavalry	22 Jul 1856	8 Sep 1860
13	John F. Reynolds	1841	Captain 3rd Artillery	8 Sep 1860	25 Jun 1861
14	Christopher C. Augur	1843	Major 13th Infantry	26 Aug 1861	5 Dec 1861
15	Kennor Garrard	1851	Captain 5th Cavalry	5 Dec 1861	25 Sep 1862
16	Henry B. Clitz	1845	Major 12th Infantry	23 Oct 1862	4 Jul 1864
17	John C. Tidball	1848	Captain 2nd Artillery	10 Jul 1864	22 Sep 1864
18	Henry M. Black	1847	Major 7th Infantry	22 Sep 1864	1 Jul 1870
19	Emory Upton	1861	Lt Col 1st Artillery	1 Jul 1870	30 Jun 1875
20	Thomas H. Neill	1847	Lt Col 6th Cavalry	1 Jul 1875	30 Jun 1879
21	Henry M. Lazelle	1855	Major 1st Infantry	1 Jul 1879	4 Aug 1882
22	Henry C. Hasbrouck	May 1861	Captain 4th Artillery	22 Aug 1882	1 Feb 1888
23	Hamilton S. Hawkins	–	Major 10th Infantry	1 Feb 1888	1 Sep 1892
24	Samuel M. Mills	1865	Captain 5th Artillery	1 Sep 1892	15 Jun 1897
25	Otto L. Hein	1870	Captain 1st Cavalry	15 Jun 1897	15 Jun 1901

No.	Name	Rank	Year		
26	Charles G. Treat	Captain 7th Artillery	1882	15 Jun 1901	15 Jun 1905
27	Robert L. Howze	Captain 6th Cavalry	1888	15 Jun 1905	1 Feb 1909
28	Frederick W. Sibley	Major 2nd Cavalry	1874	1 Feb 1909	19 Jan 1911
29	Fred W. Sladen	Major 11th Infantry	1890	19 Jan 1911	23 Jan 1914
30	Morton F. Smith	Captain 20th Infantry	1895	3 Apr 1914	16 Jun 1916
31	Guy V. Henry	Captain 13th Cavalry	1898	16 Jun 1916	6 Sep 1918
32	Jens Bugge	Colonel, US Army	1895	8 Nov 1918	17 July 1919
33	Robert M. Danford	Captain Field Artillery	1904	20 Aug 1919	1 Jul 1923
34	Merch B. Stewart	Colonel Infantry	1896	1 Jul 1923	23 Mar 1926
35	Campbell B. Hodges	Major Infantry	1903	15 Apr 1926	25 Mar 1929
36	Robert C. Richardson	Lt Col Cavalry	1904	26 Mar 1929	13 Jun 1933
37	Simon B. Buckner, Jr.	Lt Col Infantry	1908	13 Jun 1933	30 Jun 1936
38	Dennis E. McCunniff	Lt Col Infantry	1913	1 Jul 1936	30 Jun 1937
39	Charles W. Ryder	Lt Col Infantry	1915	1 Jul 1937	15 Jan 1941
40	Frederick A. Irving	Lt Col Infantry	Apr 1917	15 Jan 1941	25 Feb 1942
41	Philip E. Gallaghor	Lt Col Infantry	Jun 1918	25 Feb 1942	5 Nov 1943
42	George Honnen	Brigadier General	1920	6 Nov 1943	30 Jan 1946
43	Gerald J. Higgins	Brigadier General	1934	30 Jan 1948	18 Jun 1948
44	Paul D. Harkins	Colonel Cavalry	1929	15 Jun 1948	10 Jun 1951
45	John K. Waters	Colonel Armor	1931	11 Jun 1951	19 Jul 1952
46	John H. Michaelis	Brigadier General	1936	1 Aug 1952	10 Aug 1954
47	Edwin J. Messinger	Brigadier General	1931	1 Sep 1954	19 Apr 1956
48	John T. Throckmorton	Brigadier General	1935	19 Apr 1956	31 Aug 1959
49	Charles W.G. Rich	Brigadier General	1935	31 Aug 1959	30 Jun 1961
50	Richard G. Stilwell	Brigadier General	1938	1 Jul 1961	9 Mar 1963
51	Michael S. Davison	Brigadier General	1939	9 Mar 1963	19 Mar 1965
52	Richard P. Scott	Brigadier General	1941	17 Apr 1965	20 Aug 1967
53	Bernard W. Rogers	Brigadier General	1943	15 Sep 1967	22 Sep 1969
54	Sam S. Walker	Brigadier General	1946	15 Oct 1969	17 Sep 1972
55	Philip R. Reir	Brigadier General	1949	17 Sep 1972	13 Apr 1975
56	Walter F. Ulmer, Jr.	Brigadier General	1952	15 Apr 1975	7 Jan 1977
57	John C. Bard	Brigadier General	1954	11 Jan 1977	

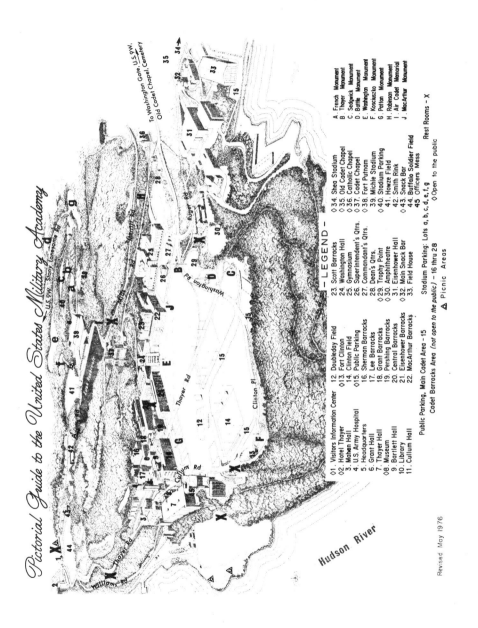

Pictorial Guide to the United States Military Academy

119